THE
FIGHT

THE FIGHT

MY BATTLE WITH DEPRESSION

CHRISTOPHER BUSSARD

gatekeeper press

Columbus, Ohio

The Fight: My Battle With Depression

Published by Gatekeeper Press
2167 Stringtown Rd, Suite 109
Columbus, OH 43123-2989
www.GatekeeperPress.com

ISBN (paperback): 9781642375688
Library of Congress Control Number: 2019935215

Cover design by Jones House Creative

Printed in the United States of America

ACKNOWLEDGMENTS

I have been working on this book in one form or another for many years. Although I have kept it relatively quiet, many people have unknowingly had a large influence on the final product. Since this book is about my life and struggles, trying to remember everyone who has impacted me for the better would be impossible. But I will do my best to acknowledge those who have helped me during the process, and those who inspired me throughout the creation of this book.

Thank you Brian Hays for supporting me and inspiring me. Without you, I would not have had the drive to complete this book. You gave me the encouragement and confidence that there are people out there who would benefit from what I have to say. You have also shown me what it means to be a good father and husband.

After I finished writing, I was at a loss for what steps to take next. I wanted to check with someone I admire and trust greatly, so I spoke with Shawn Stark to see if she knew of a good book editor, and she did. Thank you Shawn for putting me in touch with Darren Thornberry. Darren not only did a fantastic job editing, but he also guided me through the process. And thank you Darren for going above my expectations. You definitely turned this book into something I am proud of. Thanks to Matt Jones of Jones House Creative for working so hard on the cover. I wasn't sure what I was looking for, but you perfectly captured the essence of my story.

I dedicated a chapter to good friends and the impact they have made on me. Not everyone who has impacted my life made it into the book, but this book would not be what it is without them. Thank you Brian Hastey for always being someone I can count on and for showing me what a dedicated friend looks like. Thanks to Ben Carter for being there when I needed someone at the drop of a hat. Thank you Josh Schmidt for your words of encouragement, more than once, when I was going through some of the hardest times in my life. Thank you Jeff Schuppe for always being a good friend and someone I can turn to, whether you are just lending an ear, giving me good advice, or hanging out and providing good company. You also gave me the encouragement I needed to publish this book.

My family tree looks more like raspberry bushes that have intertwined than an actual tree. Because of this, I can't thank everyone individually, but thanks to all my family members. I wouldn't be where—or who—I am without you. But there are those who I must thank individually. Thanks to my mom, Terry, for making me into the man I am. You encouraged me when I needed encouragement, comforted me when I needed comfort, and toughened me up when I needed a dose of reality. Thanks to my dad, Bob (or Rob, or whatever it is this week), for teaching me so many things throughout the years, whether it's your work ethic, how to provide for and pass down good memories to your children, or any number of things I don't have room to write about here. And thank you, Ryan, for being a good big brother. You were always there to protect me. Not just to pull me out of a swimming pool, but whenever I needed you.

The person I need to thank the most is my wife, Molly. Thank you for always being there when I need you. Thank you for loving me when I'm not easy to be around. Thank you for supporting me when I am discouraged. Thank you for being such a loving wife and mother. Thank you for encouraging me during each stage of writing this book. I could not have completed it without you. Thank you for everything you do. Thank you for being you.

1

Stories tend to start from the beginning, and my story isn't any different, though I would like to think I'm more of an exception than a rule. I have spent most of my life wishing I was normal. The argument is made that normal really doesn't exist, and everyone is different. But I think that perspective comes from someone on the inside looking out. My point of view is from the outside looking in. And it sure looks nice and cozy in there when a blizzard comes at you from out of nowhere.

From as early as kindergarten I knew I was different than other people, but I had no idea why or what that meant. It was my first interaction with larger groups of children, or anyone other than family, for that matter, and I was starting to notice I wasn't the same as the other kids. I thought I was mentally slower than other kids my age, and that continued well beyond kindergarten. I saw how they behaved and wondered why I didn't act the way they did. I sat in silence as the other kids answered the teacher correctly and I didn't even understand the question. All the other children knew how to spell their names by the end of the year, but I still didn't know how to write "Christopher," so all my papers had my alias, "Chis," written at the top.

Children often recognize when things are not right or when something doesn't belong. I felt that the abnormality within me was out of place, and that I may not be welcome among my peers. Since I was under the impression I was slow, I had to disguise who I truly was for fear that my parents would have me held back. And nobody wants to be required to repeat kindergarten.

Starting school was terrifying. I stood in line with the other children, dreading the school day starting. I would rather have been anywhere else, including at home eating cooked peas. It wasn't just on the first day or the first week, but always. Each time my mother dropped me off at school I had a meltdown, and some events were worse than others. This was chalked up to me not wanting to be away from my mom, and I soon began to adapt, but I continued to wonder why I was so different. To this day, I become incredibly overwhelmed when going somewhere new or unfamiliar, causing me to sweat uncontrollably. But more on that later.

Against my will, I continued to attend school, which in retrospect was probably the right decision on the part of my parents. I had been in kindergarten for a while, and our teacher had an assignment for us, but preceding the assignment, she explained what "food for thought" meant. It didn't register. What the heck did that mean? How were the words "food" and "thought" supposed to go together? How was I supposed to pay attention to what she was saying? She was talking about something that made no sense to me, but I couldn't get over the fact that she just told us we had homework. Now I had become preoccupied with worry because we had an assignment, and I didn't know how to do homework yet. I was only in kindergarten.

Now she was past explaining "food for thought" and I couldn't figure out how food could get into my brain. She had moved on to explaining our assignment, which was to go home and cut out a newspaper headline fitting the category and bring it to school to paste on the poster board labeled "Food for Thought" at the top. She also had two other boards with other labels on top, and the assignment was the same for each. I have no recollection of what the others were because I was too busy trying to comprehend how my brain could digest food.

I gazed around the class to see if the other students were as baffled as I was, but everyone else appeared to comprehend the assignment. My worst fear was confirmed. I was way behind the other children. I would fake my way through.

I went home and explained to my mom that I had a homework assignment and I needed to cut out some newspaper headlines. She read some headlines to me and I selected some to take to school. The next day I arrived at school, assignment in hand. When the teacher asked for them, I turned mine in, hoping somehow they would fit the category and I wouldn't have to explain anything. She took my headlines, pasted them on her poster board, and moved on to the next kid. Success!

As I got older, the difference in the way I thought became more apparent, but I learned to mimic the behavior of others as I interacted with them. My behavior wasn't just altered at school or around my friends, but around my family as well. (I was many years into adulthood when my mother admitted that she had no idea I wasn't who I appeared to be on the outside until my senior year in high school. That's when she'd felt the urge to come to check on me and found the real me, much to my dismay.)

Around third grade, I developed a routine when I went to church with my dad and stepmom. Each Sunday I insisted that I join my parents in the sanctuary. My dad insisted that I go to my Sunday school class. I broke down crying, and my dad brought me to class.

We walked into the classroom, my dad dragging me by the hand while I was screaming and crying. The teacher told me I could be her helper if I stayed in the class and stopped crying. Reluctantly I agreed, partially because I knew my dad wouldn't bring me back with him anyway and I wanted to be the teacher's helper, but mostly because I knew the other kids were watching me and I didn't want this kind of attention.

One of the mornings while we were going through our routine, I heard a little girl, also being dropped off, ask her parents why I was acting like that. I knew my behavior wasn't okay. I knew the other kids didn't have this same fear of separating from their family. But I couldn't help it. My fear overtook me. I felt as though I was watching myself and had no control over my own actions. But I had no idea why.

In certain situations we are left to believe we are alone, without companionship, and without anyone from the outside understanding what we are going through. It's helpful to tell ourselves that we have it so much harder than anyone else, and nobody else could comprehend how we feel on the inside. Our own struggles are unfathomable, and if others could see what we are going through, they wouldn't complain about their lives so much. I thought about this more as I continued through life.

I got older. I moved on with school and continued to fake my way through. I mimicked the behavior of my older brother and of the other kids, hoping to blend in. Every day brought more fear. Fear of being called on by the teacher. Fear of being called out in front of the class for not knowing what I was doing. Fear of someone finding out that I was a fraud. Instead of speaking up when I was unsure, instead of being assertive, I taught myself to adapt. I taught myself to blend in. I had become a social chameleon.

I followed my older brother everywhere and attempted to take on his behavior. I dressed the way he dressed and attempted to enjoy the things he enjoyed. I even had a pair of MC Hammer pants. Although mine weren't as baggy as my brother's, they were still cool. I wore them in hopes of taking on my brother's persona. And maybe even get the dance right. I wasn't convinced about the pants, but I really did like his music. I don't know how many times I listened to my *Please Hammer, Don't Hurt 'Em* cassette, but I'm surprised the tape didn't become lodged in the cassette player and break beyond repair.

My adaptive behavior continued and I found a few things that I truly liked doing. Not just because I saw someone else having fun and I wished I could share in their happiness. These were activities I actually looked forward to and that required the majority of my concentration. I also took pride in the fact that there were some things other kids were too afraid to do, but I wasn't. I probably should have learned when I fractured my wrist in two places going off a jump on my snowboard, but sometimes I don't learn quickly enough.

When I was a freshman in high school, my brother and I took a day trip to Copper Mountain with our church. We ascended the mountain with a few of our friends, intent on getting as many runs in as possible. We forged our way through the trees in search of the perfect jump. A promising prospect showed itself to us on one of our first runs. A well-groomed path appeared to the left of the main artery and weaved its way through the trees. We came to a stop atop a steep decline just before the path lurched back skyward to the apex of the jump and disappeared to nowhere.

One of our brave, more experienced friends volunteered to go first. He stood up, twisted his board ninety degrees so that he was in line with the path, and off he went. As he was airborne, only a few feet above the top of the jump, we heard an ominous scream that one would think came from the soundtrack of a horror movie. Much to our surprise, he appeared to have survived the landing, which was confirmed when we heard his faint voice echoing from the bottom to take it slow.

One after the other, our friends slowly made their way down the path and off the jump, each with their own auditioning scream for the upcoming horror movie. Next was my turn. But why should I take it slow? I was always the first to do anything big. I was the one to jump off the neighbor's deck to the not-so-forgiving lawn below. I was the one called on to catch the snake when everyone else found some excuse not to. Why should this be different?

The jump rose about four feet from the path on the uphill side. This did not mirror itself on the downhill side. It was later explained to me that I was probably about five feet above the jump at my highest point. This jump was designed with the idea to go straight up from the launch and come straight down the other side. That was not my approach. As I heaved myself off the top, I soon realized why it was recommended to go slow. I gazed down at the icy snow below. The hillside resembled a "J" and, had I approached properly, I would have continued unscathed to its crook and then down the rest of the slope. But at my peak I bypassed the optimal landing spot, and the closer I got to the ground that was ten feet below the top of the jump, the icy run began to angle ever-so-slightly back toward me. I landed with the gracefulness of a belly flop from the high dive.

Every square inch on the bottom of my snowboard smacked the ground simultaneously, which is not optimal. My knees absorbed as much of the impact as possible, but the force was more than I could have expected my lower extremities to take. As gravity continued to perform as expected, I reached my right hand to the ground to brace myself (also not recommended at this velocity). Immediately I felt a sharp pain in my wrist, but surprisingly it appeared to be intact. As a companion poked and prodded at my wrist, he assured me it was only sprained. I cradled the injured appendage with my left arm as I braced it against my chest and proceeded cautiously down the run toward the medical building, leaving my ego on the mountain. Unfortunately, X-rays showed that my wrist was fractured.

At thirteen years old, watching your older brother fall while jumping down seven concrete steps on his skateboard should make you second guess attempting it. I took it as a challenge. Perhaps I would have been a little more cautious had my snowboarding incident preceded it, but at this point I still lacked a sense of fragility.

The middle school was one of our regular skating spots. It included sets of three, five, seven, and nine stairs. The sidewalk we used to obtain enough speed to propel ourselves sufficiently down the stairs abutted the school. We would start parallel with the school, and after a quick ninety-degree turn we had little room to regain the proper composure in order to prepare ourselves for the upcoming leap, so we often were not as balanced as we would have preferred. But that did not deter us from attempting the trick anyway.

We used the set of three stairs to practice kickflips, heelflips, and my favorite—the backside heelflip. Once we were comfortable with the set of three, we moved on to the set of five and eventually the set of seven. This is where we challenged each other and ourselves. The sidewalk leading to the set of seven stairs continued from the corner of the building, negating the need for the quick turn prior to the drop. This allowed more time for preparation and, consequently, more speed.

One day, we set out to accomplish something spectacular. After falling several times, I probably should have given up. Whether it was the competition with my brother, with our friends, or just within myself, I wasn't going to give up. I can't recall which one of us landed our trick du jour first, but I'm pretty sure we stayed in front of the middle school, taking turns finding new ways to tuck and roll as we fell, until we all had at least one successful run. But my boosted sense of accomplishment and self-pride fizzled away like a bottle rocket; once it's gone, all that remains is the image of what once was, briefly burned into your retina.

Much like skateboarding and snowboarding, football helped mold me into my future self. The first time I put on football pads and ran full speed into another kid, I was hooked. There is something about the crack of shoulder pads and the smell of the field that will forever be ingrained into my memory. The football field was a place I could forget about who I really was. Even though I was the skinniest kid on the team, I started out as a lineman. I would stare down kids much bigger than I was and prepare for hand-to-hand combat. Once the ball was snapped, it was a battle of sheer willpower. I wouldn't give up until the whistle blew or they were on their back. I wasn't thinking about how different I was or wonder why I wasn't like everyone else. For that moment, we were all on the same playing field.

I held onto the belief that some day I would be a professional athlete. I imagined myself as a role model for young children all over the country. But the same way a single weed can grow and multiply, taking over an entire garden, who I really was would eventually take over who I wanted to be. It would keep me on the field only long enough to hold onto the hope. The dream of playing in the NFL would remain just that—a dream. However, my compassion for others will forever be a part of me.

During my brief stint in college, I was shaken to the depth of my very being, and the failing dream of who I wanted to be and the reality of who I was met head on. But this collision resulted in a product I never imagined.

I was preparing for class on the morning of September 11, 2001, when I overheard the TV in the dorm room next to mine. I listened intently, hoping to recognize what movie the guy next door was watching. But the more I listened, I realized he wasn't watching any movie; it was the morning news. I gathered my books for class, tossed them into my backpack, and rushed to my friend's dorm down the hall since he had a television in his room. I stood in disbelief as we watched the second jet crash into Tower 1 of the Twin Towers. This was one of those moments in life where our minds refuse to accept as reality the events playing out in front of us.

My first class would be starting soon, so I went to the cafeteria to grab some breakfast. A group of us gathered around a table, not saying a word, as we continued to watch the morning news. Much to our dismay, classes continued and we all sat in our first class with little productivity. All we could think about was getting out of class to see what the latest updates were and who was responsible for such an atrocity. We all went on with our normal activities, but we were only going through the motions. Teachers didn't want to teach and students didn't want to learn.

I kept up to speed on world events as I finished the semester, but I had an ever-growing feeling that I wasn't where I needed to be. I had no desire to continue with my classes, but finished anyway because I refuse to quit what I have started. But even football was beginning to lose its luster. Nothing seemed to be what it was before. Without any other plan, I did not return the next semester. I decided to take the next couple months traveling to the west coast in hopes of finding myself there. Instead, I ended up even more lost than when I started.

After the events of September 11, there was a sense of unity in the United States. We saw each other as fellow Americans and neighbors, not just as that person you see in passing and will never see again. And we looked at first responders in a way we never had before. If you wanted to watch a documentary on police, fire, or EMS workers, you just had to flip through the channels and you would come across one.

After I returned from my west coast trip, I was watching one of these documentaries and something hit me in the deepest part of my soul. The first responders who ran into the Twin Towers were part of something greater than themselves. They lived and died with a sense of purpose. They had the hope they could make a difference. Whether it was helping an old lady who fell or pulling multiple people out of a skyscraper before it crumbled to the ground, they were making a difference. This is what I wanted to do. I wanted to be a firefighter.

I moved back in with my dad and stepmom, hoping to get my feet back on the ground and my life back in order. I had a new feeling of hope in purpose, but

I didn't know how to go about becoming a firefighter. Did I need to get certifications first? What certifications did I need? Where do I get them? I would have to start researching this when I had time. We still had the old dial-up Internet access that took an entire evening to load a single website, so I had to dedicate some research time between looking for temporary jobs.

Since this was when looking for a job meant going from one business to another asking for applications, I was out all morning. After I had an acceptable stack of applications to work on, I went home. My parents let me know there was some mail on the kitchen counter for me. It was a postcard addressed to the "current resident" from our fire department. It said they were looking for volunteers, no experience necessary. Sometimes I think God's timing is amazing, or maybe He is just showing off.

On September 12, 2002, I turned my application in to the fire department for the position of volunteer firefighter. I was informed that I would proceed through the hiring process, and if I passed each step, I would be sworn in as a volunteer in December. I had no idea what to expect when they told me I would be going through their oral boards. I found myself in front of a panel of five firefighters grilling me on my response to each question they asked. No matter what answer I came up with, I would have been wrong. The key was to stick by your original decision and explain why it was the correct decision to make.

I didn't do much to prepare for the physical ability test other than exercise, since I had no idea what I should do. We began by ascending and descending the 85-foot aerial ladder. We pulled hose. We carried tools up the stairs, through the building, and back down the other set of stairs. We pulled the rescue dummy across the front pad, and so on. And we were timed. Once we finished, we were instructed to put on a full set of gear as they blacked out our masks. We then proceeded to crawl our way around the building as the instructors questioned us on how to get out. This part is designed to see if you can keep your cool in this situation. I had no idea how I would react before I began, but apparently I did well enough, or at least didn't panic too much, and I passed the physical assessment. Once I began testing for career positions on other fire departments, I would find this was child's play compared to some of the other assessments.

In December 2002, I got sworn in as a probationary firefighter, and my training began. The first year they sent us through fire academy with a neighboring fire department. We then went through HazMat training, and eventually EMT class. Once we had those certifications, and after our first year was over, we were sworn in as firefighters.

When I started, the fire department consisted of only volunteers. But like everything else, it changed with time and we hired a few members. I applied with each hiring process, but never made the final cut. I applied to as many departments as I could, but without any luck. After ten years as a volunteer, I began to wonder if this is really what I was meant to do for a profession. Could it be that I was only meant to pursue this as a volunteer? Was there something else I was supposed to do for a career? When I started to lose hope, I finally got hired on by the department I put so much time and effort into, in the community where I grew up.

Satisfaction in what we have does not come easy. We always want what we don't have, or more of what we do. Life is like pouring water into a cup with a hole in the bottom. I hold onto my delusions that I can change the world. I say that it will be worth it to change the world for one person, but that's not true. Waving to children from the fire engine or giving them a tour of the station, taking care of an elderly man as he struggles to breathe, or shaking hands with the Fire Chief as he hands me a life-saving award gives a brief moment of satisfaction. But my cup will never be full. I want to do more. I will try to do what I can to give others hope, but I will never be satisfied. It's the feeling that nothing I do will ever be good enough.

I've spent my entire life struggling with depression, anxiety, and obsessive-compulsive disorder. It consumes me, every hour of every day. It dictates my thoughts and my actions. I am a slave to the irrational notions of my own mind. This is the cross I bear. Every day I wonder why I am the way I am. Why would God allow me to have this debilitating disease? If He wants me to follow him, why would he make it so hard? But then I think I am asking the wrong questions.

I struggle with what it means to follow God while suffering from a mental illness. It hurts me to see others with this same disorder. And it pains me to watch as people are overwhelmed by it, and succumb to the unimaginable power of its evil. So I am left wondering what I can do about it. How can I reach others who suffer as I do and feel there is no hope? How can I give them hope?

I can write.

For more than half of my life I wanted to write a book, but discouragement is often stronger than desire. And talent may be an illusion as delusions of grandeur fill my head. As I begin to write, something whispers to me, explaining how nothing I write will reach the people I would like. I enjoy writing nonetheless. Typically I write short stories, most of which are fictional, but I decided to write the story of my life. It doesn't end with, "They lived happily ever after," and there are no amazing revelations that change my life forever. It's a story of reality. A story of perseverance. A story of hope. A hope that maybe I will have a positive impact on someone. A hope that someday I will hear my Creator say to me, "Well done." A hope that there is hope. A hope that I can give someone hope when they feel there is none left.

2

Fire academy was finished, and I found myself in EMT class. I was working as a server in a pizza restaurant and started pulling shifts at the fire station as a volunteer. I was beginning to feel like I had my foot in the door and would soon be on my way to being an adult. It was about time since I was already twenty-two, but perhaps now I would be able to pull my own weight.

A good friend of mine from high school was on break from college and came back to town. Todd is a genuine, good guy and always fun to be around, so I was happy to meet up with him. He's a good person, but Todd always has a joke or two to play on someone. A case in point is our church's annual weeklong high school camp, which we attended several times. One year Todd and I found several bricks scattered around our cabin, which we arranged in a certain way and set on the bench in front of the cabin. The bricks were shaped like octagons, with one of the sides being replaced by a square protrusion, so arranging them took some time. The finished product appeared very similar to a person sitting on the bench. If we only had a mop head, we could make it into a woman. Found one!

The figure no way looked like an actual woman, and her appearance was quite comical. I'm pretty sure we even named her, though I have no idea what it was. We wished we could have made her stand up, but she wouldn't have been able to support her own weight. I was quite content letting her sit on the bench in front, but Todd had other plans. Before we knew it, our statue made her way into another friend's sleeping bag. He didn't find it as hilarious as we did.

So when Todd came back into town, I jumped at the chance to get together. And our meeting would send my life down a path I wasn't expecting. He let me know our friend Jon was working at a restaurant about a half hour away. The three of us met up maybe once after high school, and I had hoped this would be a pattern of many future gatherings, but sometimes life gets in the way. Jon was happy to see the two of us when we showed up at the restaurant, and we planned to meet after he got off work. Much to our surprise, Jon was getting married in a couple weeks, and he told us he wanted us to be there.

Todd had to get back to Illinois to continue college, but I let Jon know I would be happy to attend.

Jon and his fiancée had a DJ lined up for the wedding, but due to a family emergency the day before, he had to cancel. The company didn't have any available DJs in the state of Colorado for the next day, so they contacted the next closest location: Kearney, Nebraska. If you've never heard of Kearney, don't worry, you're not the only one. It sits in the middle of the state on I-80. Five hours west is Denver, and if you head the opposite direction, it's about two hours to Lincoln. It's a college town, and like the town where I went to college, the population pretty much doubles when school is in session.

Molly was standing in the office when the call came in requesting a DJ for the wedding; her boss answered the phone. "Hang on a second." He put the phone down and looked at Molly. "You want to go to Colorado tomorrow?"

"Sure."

The day of the wedding I drove to Jon's house and rode with him to the hotel where they would later have the reception. Jon's parents rented several rooms for the family and groomsmen to stay for the night. The plan was for me to ride with his family to the church and then back to the hotel. The next day they would drive me back to their house where I'd left my car.

It was good to catch up with Jon as we drove the half-hour north to the hotel. I wished him good luck as he left for the church and I hitched a ride with his parents. There wasn't as much for us to catch up on, but it was nice to see them again, too. After the ceremony we all headed back to the hotel for the reception, and I found myself sitting with another friend from high school and his family. He was probably my best friend growing up, but after school we didn't keep in touch.

I was enjoying catching up with more friends, but I caught a glimpse of the DJ and couldn't pay much attention to anything else. I wondered why it took me so long to notice her as I sat at the table and watched her work. Dressing in black dress pants and a black, button-up, long sleeve dress shirt shouldn't normally draw someone's attention. But she had a beautiful familiarity I couldn't get past. Her blonde hair was pulled up in a ponytail, revealing beauty enhanced by the rainbow of her multicolored blue, green, and brown eyes.

The longer I sat, the more I attempted to draw up enough courage to go talk to her. The guests at the table were my own personal pep squad. It was time. I had to act. I stood up, gathered my strength, and began to saunter in her direction. But I was foiled by the best man. He beat me to the punch and I sulked back to the table with my tail between my legs as he spoke to the DJ. I was five seconds too late.

The night went on and I felt like the creepy stalker you would see in a movie, who constantly stares at a woman without blinking. I watched as Molly entertained with several games and instructed the crowd on dancing with the proper disco moves such as the lawn-mower and the shopping cart. She explained a game she wanted to play with everyone, but she needed chairs. And then I saw her approaching. Was she coming to talk to me? My heart began to race. She stood in front of me, pointed to the empty chair at my side, and asked if it was available. As I gathered my jaw from the floor, my friends congregated at the table explained to her that the chair was available. She snatched it up and walked away. Foiled again.

Molly began to gather patrons who were willing to partake in whatever cruel game she concocted. I must have blacked out for a second because, the next thing I knew, I was sitting in one of the chairs in front of the crowd. Somehow she persuaded me to join in the festivities, which is quite the feat because I avoid being the center of attention with the same lack of self worth as when a dog avoids looking you in the eye while he's being scolded for getting into the garbage.

I was now participating in a game similar to musical chairs. But in this inhumane version, contestants must retrieve an object from the crowd and return to their seats, at which time they find one chair has been removed, allowing all but the last person to find a seat. The first task: a woman's shoe. Mission accomplished. As we continued, we were given the task to not only find lipstick, but to also apply it to our lips. I eyeballed my friend's mother who was sitting at the table I was recently a member of until I was unwillingly dragged away. I was sure to get a seat since our table was right in front. Molly called out "go" and off we went. I ran to my friend's mom, applied her lipstick to my lips, and ran back to find a seat. I was promptly disqualified when the DJ decided the quantity of lipstick on my lips was not sufficient for me to continue. I knew it; she hated me.

Dancing and games proceeded throughout the night, and future attempts by me to speak to the DJ were thwarted by the best man getting there first. The night wound down and the reception came to an end. I picked myself up, accepted my defeat as another example of my passiveness getting the best of me, and headed back to the hotel room to change my clothes. I put on the cargo pants and t-shirt I wore prior to the wedding and headed back downstairs to the hotel lobby. Jon's family was gathered around the oversized fireplace in the lounge. I grabbed a drink from the bar and sat in an empty chair among Jon's family members in an effort to pretend to be a part of the gathering. I spoke as few words as necessary, and only when prompted by someone asking how things were going and what I had been up to.

We are usually given one chance in any given situation to do what we think is right. If we choose incorrectly, or fail to make a decision, we live with the consequences for the remainder of our lives. Very rarely are we given a second chance at a passing failure. Perhaps my previous experiences don't always predict the future, and I felt like maybe I had another chance when I heard a familiar voice requesting attention from the room.

I looked up to see the DJ at the perimeter of our congregation. She had changed her clothes and was now wearing a brown plaid, button-up, three-quarter-sleeve shirt with the sleeves rolled up just above her elbows. If possible, it enhanced what I thought could quite possibly be the most beautiful person I'd ever seen. "I've never been to this town," she called out to the group. "Does anyone want to come with me to see what it's all about?" Could this be my second chance?

Courage comes in many forms. I sat there and collected everything I had from within, gathered all my courage, and with the overwhelming confidence of a boy asking a girl to prom, I slowly raised my hand into the air as though I was back in school and the teacher just asked who the seventh president of the United States was. It's a wonder my kids were ever born.

Since I needed a little liquid courage to allow me to converse with her, Molly drove us around that night. We spent the next several hours in one continuous conversation. There weren't any awkward pauses where one of us tried to find another subject to talk about in order to fill the silence. Once I became a little more comfortable, I put my arm around her and pointed out that she was at the perfect height where the top of her shoulder nestled into my armpit, as if we were two puzzle pieces that we finally discovered could match up together.

We spent the next couple of days together. We drove to the mountains. I brought her to Boulder Falls. We each later admitted to having the feeling that we had known each other our entire lives. When she called her friend in Nebraska to let her know she would be staying in Colorado a couple more days, I was touched that her friend cared so much about her, pointing out that Molly didn't really know me at all. But there wasn't any way for Molly to make her friend understand that we did in fact know each other as if we were once childhood friends reunited after a decade apart.

The night before she headed back to Nebraska, I spent our entire dinner together giving Molly a list of reasons why she needed to move to Colorado. To top it off, I had a friend in need of a roommate. By the time we left the restaurant I had her convinced. She left the next morning, and a week later she came back again to visit. I was still living with my dad, and the memory of seeing her car driving down the street and pulling in front of the house is ingrained in my brain. I remember the excitement I felt just seeing her step out of the car. I keep this memory in permanent storage in my brain, and each time I open the file it is as though I am reliving that moment. But the more files I store away, the less I find myself returning to this one to remind myself of how lucky I am.

I am not an easy person to deal with, and I'm not good with relationships. I don't communicate well, and I find friendships hard to maintain. But for some reason the piece to my puzzle that I felt had been missing for so long seems to understand me. At least the best that can be expected, seeing as most of the time I can't seem to understand myself. She stuck by me in my roughest times and helped guide me through my darkest nights. After only three years together, she agreed to marry me. When you find someone who has seen you at the capacity of the wreckage you are capable of being and loves you anyway, you don't let them go. Plus, I figured we should get married before she realized she's too good for me.

In our many years together, more than a decade of marriage, and having three children, we have accumulated a lifetime of memories. I could probably write a book with the sole topic of our adventures together. The story behind each broken down car would yield its own chapter. But to relieve us all of the side story caused by my mind wandering down memory lane, I will leave those journeys for a story yet to be told. Our story continues to be written, with all its ups and downs.

As I continued to test for career positions with fire departments in Colorado, Molly always stuck by me and encouraged me. She remained positive each time I received a rejection letter and assured me that my time would come. I obtained different certifications, which each required time away from home, but Molly kept encouraging me. My fire department pager would go off when we got a call, and immediately Molly would say, "Be safe." There may have been a few times I should have stayed home, knowing other members would beat me there and hop on the rig before I arrived, and I would just be hanging out waiting for them to get back. This left Molly alone at home as my dinner got cold.

When Molly was due with our first child, I was scheduled to work a night shift at the station. It was agreed beforehand that if she went into labor, I would need to leave. Several hours before my shift was going to start, we got a call for a structure fire. I looked at Molly, "You're not going into labor, are you?" Before she fully assured me she wasn't, I was heading out the door.

I got to the station and hopped on a rig just as they were about to pull out of the station. The fire started in one house, extended to the multiple vehicles parked outside, and then to the neighbor's garage. Needless to say, we were going to be there a while. By the time we were finished, it was past time for my shift to start, and we would still have to clean up when we got back. I called Molly to see how she was doing, and the baby still was not on her way. Then I explained the real reason for my call. "Can you bring my stuff to the station for me since I won't be coming home tonight?" I tried to be as apologetic as I could, but I'm sure I didn't come off as feeling too bad. So nine-month-pregnant Molly gathered my overnight bag and headed for the station. When she got there she was more interested in hearing about the fire than complaining about her swollen ankles and having to drive to the station when she was extremely pregnant. These are the things I take for granted. Logically I know I should appreciate how well she treats me. But the part of me that blurs the lines between perception and reality hinders me from accepting what I truly have.

For some reason, my wife continues to stick by me in spite of the fact that most of what I do should cause her to, at a minimum, smack me in the back of the head with a frying pan. I know how I am, and most of the time I can't stand me. But I'm stuck with myself and I don't have any say in the matter. It wasn't optional. Since I've lived with myself my entire life, I've sort of gotten used to my strange behaviors. My wife, however, chooses to remain by my side throughout all the good times and bad, even though it defies logic. I think she may have been a little weary after the first time my obsessive-compulsive behavior showed its ugly face, when I lost my mind after she unwittingly moved my socks when I had them right where I wanted them. She was only trying to clean up. I often wonder why she has vowed to forever love and support me. But I guess I don't see myself the way she does. Perhaps she has been sent to watch over me. Or maybe she's as crazy as I am. The jury's still out.

3

As a kid, and especially as a teenager, I focused a lot on my parents' shortcomings. As an adult, I realize being a parent is hard. There is a difficult compromise between correcting my children so they grow up to be responsible adults, and letting them be kids and have fun. I frequently remind them, and myself, that I discipline them because I love them. If I did not care about their future, I wouldn't care what they do today.

Love is an amazing thing. When you fall in love with someone, you can't imagine loving anyone else as much as you love them. When you have a child, you begin to understand. It is a love completely different than any other. But you can't imagine having another child because you can't fathom loving another child as much as the first. When your second child is born, you get it. Love does not divide; it multiplies. When you have multiple children, you look at each and wonder how it's possible to love each of them with all your heart. I have three kids, and I am amazed at the ever-increasing capacity of my own heart to love. It always finds room for more. I look at one of my children and have no idea how I could love anyone else that much, and then enters another. I simply can't explain it to anyone else who is not in the same situation and expect them to understand. But I find this amazingly similar to believing in God. I can explain to someone how and why I feel the way I do, but until you are in the same situation, you cannot comprehend.

Our first child was two and a half, and I sat in my chair trying to rest my back after I tweaked it playing basketball with the church. I remember waking up when my daughter came to give me a kiss before going upstairs to take a nap. I have a vague recollection of Molly going upstairs after that for a while. I'm not sure how long it had been, but I woke up when she was on her way back down.

"Do you remember how you told me it was still too early to find out?" she asked, semi-smug. "Well, it's positive." I swiveled my chair enough to see her as she came down the stairs, holding a pregnancy test in her hand.

Before Molly was pregnant with our daughter, she told me that she would never tell me over the phone when she found out she was pregnant. The problem with that is when she found out she was pregnant with our first child, we were working opposite schedules and we wouldn't be seeing each other for at least another day and a half. At that time I was working twelve-hour days, and when I got home on a typical day she would already have left for work. We saw each other in passing before I went to work again, and she wasn't going to tell me she was pregnant as I was about ready to leave.

Molly called me at the Urgent Care where I was working to tell me that she was pregnant because there was no way she would be able to wait more than a day without telling anyone. And she wasn't going to tell anyone else until she told me. When I got the call at work I had to sit down and take a break; I couldn't quit smiling.

Telling me she was pregnant while I was half asleep and in pain wasn't the way she had planned to tell me the second time around, but at least this time she was able to tell me in person. She was so excited about it, but I wasn't really in any position to jump up and down. Not that I'm the sort of person who shows excitement that way, or really in any way for that matter. I don't usually wear my emotions on my sleeve.

Over the next several months we did all the things you do to prepare for a second child. We started getting our house ready for a baby. We gave our daughter a big girl bed, and she was more than happy to give her bed to the baby. She had a transition bed, and it was currently in toddler mode so we swapped it back to a crib. When we told her we were going to have a baby, she told us all the things she was going to give and teach the baby. She explained how she would give the baby her bed, and gave us a list of her toys that she wanted to hand down. She constantly told us she was going to teach the baby to stack blocks. We told her we thought that would be very nice of her.

When it came to the doctor's appointments, we made sure I would be able to go by scheduling them when I wasn't working. I tried to make it to every appointment when Molly was pregnant with our first child, and I didn't want to miss any of them this time, either. Our daughter was thrilled to go as well, and told us each time that she wanted to listen to the baby's "heart beep."

Prior to having our daughter, we discussed whether we wanted to find out the gender of our baby, but we weren't quite sure. When it came down to it, we wanted to know and were thrilled to learn we were going to have a girl. Neither of us cared what gender the baby was. All we prayed for was a healthy baby.

This time around we knew we wanted to find out the gender. The three of us, along with the tech, packed into the room for the ultrasound. When we went in for the ultrasound with our daughter, we could tell she was a girl before the tech told us, so this time we wanted to guess. The tech took all the measurements and told us we would be having a healthy baby. When it came time, she asked if we wanted to know if this one was a boy or a girl, and we explained that we did but we wanted to guess. She maneuvered her magic video camera over my wife's jelly-covered baby belly until the ultrasound was in the appropriate position for us to attempt to identify the baby's gender. Without getting too graphic, I will just say that Molly and I belted out simultaneously, "It's a boy!" And yes, this time all we wanted was a healthy baby, but we were thrilled to find out we were having a boy. We would now have one of each, as if we were collecting something.

Molly has always suffered from migraines, and as she got further along in her pregnancy they became more frequent. I wanted to help, but the only thing I could do was spend time with our daughter so Molly could rest. She reassured me that I was being very helpful, but I always wished there was more I could do.

We continued to go to our appointments, and Molly consistently measured a week big. This wasn't unusual since she always measured a little further along than was expected, starting at the first ultrasound. The doctor continued to tell us we were going to have another big baby.

Before our daughter was born, we were told she would be a big baby as well. After two hours of my wife pushing, our daughter was finally coming out, but during the delivery the baby's shoulders got stuck. They rushed another nurse into the room and like a running back rushing for his first touchdown, she stiff-armed me as she rushed by. She pushed me aside, climbed up on the side of the bed like a diver takes to the platform, and began pushing and shoving on Molly's belly, rocking from side to side trying to manipulate our daughter enough to get her out. I wondered how a brand new baby could take such trauma.

Finally the baby was free from her entanglement, and they rushed her to the warming bed to examine her and make sure everything was fine. They got her there, and she still hadn't started crying. With me being the outwardly calm person I am, and being trained to deal with emergency situations, I remained calm. I looked at Molly and knew she was starting to worry.

"Why isn't she crying?" Molly asked, with a semi-panicked look on her face. Just after she finished asking that question, we heard the sweetest cry coming from our newborn daughter, and I saw tears of joy running down my wife's cheek. The first thing Molly wanted to do was to hold her newborn baby and spend the first few minutes together, and she wanted me to cut the umbilical cord. With all the happenings that come after a baby gets stuck in one way or another, neither of her top checklist items were accomplished.

With the second child, Molly was hoping she would be able to check off the items she missed out on the first time. She wanted to spend the first few minutes with him, and she wanted me to cut the cord. As Molly got closer to her due date, she often said that she didn't think this baby would wait until his scheduled time to come out. The doctor was concerned that since our daughter got stuck, and this baby was measuring big, he could also get stuck. We discussed the possibility of inducing early if the baby didn't come on his own merit, but they could not induce any earlier than a week before the due date.

Molly and I went home, considered our options, and discussed our concerns. We came to the conclusion that we would schedule an induction the earliest we could, and if the baby came sooner than his due date, all would be fine, but we didn't want the baby getting too big. As my wife got further along, she continued to remind me that she didn't think the baby would make it to his due date. She also felt the need to remind me that she was over being pregnant and wanted him to come out already.

I was scheduled to work until the day before the induction, but I took the rest of the week off. It was finally the day before the big day, and since I was at work, Molly took our daughter to stay with my mom while we were in the hospital. I got home and Molly called the doctor's office to confirm our induction at 7:00 the next morning. They told her she needed to call at 5:00 the morning of to make sure there was enough available staff to do the induction, and make sure they weren't busy with other deliveries. Since it had only been three years since our last child was born, we should have remembered that some people don't plan these things.

We got up nice and early the next morning and Molly called the doctor's office. They told her they had a couple of women delivering babies, and they were going to delay the induction by half an hour. There was no way we were going to be able to get to sleep at that point, so we got up and got ready for the adventure that was awaiting us. We were ready to go, but didn't have to leave for a while. It was the first time in a while we didn't have our daughter with us, and since it was just the two of us, Molly decided she wanted to go get a doughnut.

I put everything we packed the previous night into the car, locked up the house, checked everything a few more times, and we got in the car and headed to the doughnut shop. Doughnuts and coffee in hand, we sat down to enjoy what was sure to be the most relaxing time we would have for quite some time, despite the fact that Molly was extremely pregnant, which for some reason the lady working behind the counter felt the need to point out.

When it was time to go, we got back into the car and made the trek to the hospital. We reminisced about when we were going to the hospital to have our daughter. We talked about how different things were then, and how different they would be after having two children. We got to the hospital, I grabbed only the bags we needed immediately, and we headed up to labor and delivery. Molly pointed out that we were going into the building having one child and would be leaving as the parents of two.

We headed to our pre-assigned room, and since we got there at shift change, we met the nurse who would be with us for the next twelve hours. We had previously discussed what we thought the view would be like from the room, so the first thing I did was go to the window and open the curtains, which revealed a beautiful view of the snow-capped mountains. I knew Molly would not really be able to enjoy the view, but I was sure it wouldn't hurt anything. I tossed the bags on the couch and helped Molly get as comfortable as she could be.

The nurse had a student with her, and asked if it would be okay if the student started the IV. Molly explained that the only way for her to learn was to actually do it. This came as a surprise to me since she seemed quite concerned when I had to start an IV on her during her previous pregnancy. The student prepped everything to start the procedure, and I sat on the other side of the bed, trying not to be too critical or let it be obvious that I was making sure she did everything correctly. I began to have some palpitations when she wasn't setting everything up the way I would have; I took a deep breath. I wanted to start the IV myself, or at least give a word of advice, but I remained silent. I knew I wouldn't like it if someone tried to tell me how to do my job.

The student had everything neatly organized, and with the help of the nurse she got the IV started. I could relax. I wanted to give her a hard time to make Molly nervous since she's afraid of needles in the first place, but I figured this wasn't a good time for that. The student got the line secured and the fluids began to flow. They hooked Molly up to the monitors in order to make sure both she and the baby were doing well; all was good. After everything was set, they started giving her the Pitocin to start the labor process.

Several hours went by, and Molly and I tried to find things to do in our new cubby of a room. We talked about what it would be like to have a boy, we watched a movie, and did whatever else we could do to pass the time. The nurse and her student checked on us from time to time, but we were sure they were trying not to bother us too often. They checked the baby's vital signs and made sure my wife was doing well. We kept telling ourselves we would have another child by the end of the day. But as the hours went by and the end of the day neared, we wondered if the baby was going to hold out until the next day. Apparently he was more patient than we were.

After hours of anticipation, it was only a couple hours until midnight, and Molly was finally at the point where she was starting to push. We have heard the second child usually comes quicker than the first, so we figured our son would still be born before midnight. As if Molly needed any encouragement, the nurse instructed her to begin pushing. The doctor came in periodically to check on her progress, but after a couple hours, the doctor discussed with Molly and me the possibility of having to perform a cesarean. This was definitely not what my wife wanted, but she appeared to be having a harder time with this baby than she did with our daughter.

After a little over two hours of pushing, the doctor told Molly that if the baby didn't come in another half hour we would seriously need to consider having a C-section. Not quite a half hour later Molly reluctantly told the doctor, "I think we need to talk about the C-section now."

Molly was in tears as she apologized continuously to the nurse, to the doctor, and to me. She explained how she felt like a failure since she was not able to deliver the baby naturally. We told her numerous times that she didn't need to be sorry, but she still felt as though we were upset with her.

The doctor exited the room and went to prep for surgery, and the nurse explained what we needed to do. She handed me scrubs and explained what was going to happen. When they were ready, they wheeled Molly into the operating room. I felt as though they were prepping me to perform the surgery myself as I put on my gown, mask, and booties, and followed the nurse into the operating room. I sat beside my wife as everything was prepared. After what seemed like hours, but I'm sure was only a matter of minutes, they informed us they would be starting the procedure.

People were running all over the room, and I couldn't tell who the doctors were, who the nurses were, and who the techs were. I just knew they were all working hard to deliver my son. Molly and I were on one side of the sheet and couldn't see anything happening on the other. I was fine with this. I have seen many things in my life that people shouldn't have to see and have been fine with it, but no part of me wanted to witness what was going on behind that thin blue sheet.

There was a brief pause in the chaos that were the thoughts running through our minds when the doctor peered over to our side of the paper wall to inform us the C-section was a good idea. "That is a big head. No wonder he wouldn't fit." She then disappeared back to her side and continued to work.

After what seemed like another hour, the doctor told us she was starting to pull the baby out. As I sat there in anticipation I heard a little noise from my son as they extracted him from my wife's wide open abdomen. After that, we didn't hear anything. After he was delivered, the nurse passed by with my son, and I caught a glimpse of him as they carried him to the warming table. I sat in my chair waiting for the much-anticipated first cry. I remembered it taking a little while when our daughter was born, but Molly and I continued to wait. As we sat longer and longer, I could tell she was beginning to worry, but I, being the calm person that I am, wasn't concerned.

Molly was looking at me as I turned to look at her. A tear rolled down her face. "Why isn't he crying?" she asked. At that point I began to get concerned. Sometimes it takes a while, but it seemed to be a long time since they delivered my son, and he still wasn't breathing. But I knew in situations such as this, things seem to go by slower than they actually do. I rolled my chair to position myself between my wife and our son. Not wanting to let her know I was concerned, I told her it was going to be fine. I reminded her that when our daughter was born, she was concerned for the same reason.

At that point I heard the unmistakable sound of the flow of oxygen coming from behind me. When a newborn is not breathing, the first thing to do is blow pure oxygen over the baby's face. Often this will stimulate the baby's breathing reflex and they will begin to breathe on their own. We sat longer, but still did not hear any cry. I maintained confidence that everything would be fine. Then I heard a sound there is no way I could mistake. I have heard this sound many times before, but never in a situation like this. Whether I was in denial or maybe I thought I was mistaken, I whipped my head around to see for myself when I heard it.

As I turned to look toward my newborn son, I saw two nurses at the warming table hovering over him. One of the nurses was giving him artificial respirations with a bag-valve-mask. I watched for a while, turned to make sure I was between my wife and our son, and then looked back. The nurses worked with a calm sense of urgency. In this situation they knew there was an issue, but couldn't show any worry. Any outward sign of distress would cause us to panic.

I had a barrage of thoughts come to my mind as I sat there longer and longer, the nurses still giving ventilations to my son. Were we going to leave the hospital without him? How was I going to tell this to my wife? How would we explain to our three-year-old daughter that she wouldn't have a brother after all? How would we be able to face our families and explain this to them? What were things going to be like for us as a family without our son?

"Please Lord Jesus," I prayed silently. A tear rolled down my face. "Please reach down from Heaven and protect my son." I couldn't turn to look at Molly, because I knew if she saw me with tears in my eyes she would know something was going on.

Just as I finished this prayer, I heard a baby cry behind me. I never knew a baby crying could bring me so much joy. I turned and looked at Molly, and we both had tears in our eyes. Our son continued to cry as the nurses wrapped him up and showed him to us. I looked around the room at the doctors and nurses as they continued to put my wife back together, and there was a collective sigh of relief. I knew that they, just like me, didn't want to show any emotions, but were concerned.

After they rejuvenated my son, I joyfully followed the nurses to the recovery room as they carried him. What was helplessness and hopelessness was now an overwhelming sense of relief. They continued to evaluate him as they got his measurements and vital signs. They proceeded with their duties, and after their examination found no signs of trauma. Our son was just fine. The nurse handed my son to me and I sat down in the chair. My heart was happy. I gave thanks to the Holy Spirit. I sat there holding my son, and looked at all the nurses in the room. I am forever grateful to them for what they did. I know to them it was another day at work, but to us this was our life.

I look at my son, many years later, and he gives me a big grin and raises his eyebrows as if he is scheming or plotting something. I am reminded of what could have been, and how easily what we have can be taken away. I thank God for what I have. I look at my children and my wife and I remember that I need to look at what I have and not what I wish I had. I'm reminded of those who are not as fortunate, those who struggle with more difficult things. I'm reminded of those who may have gone through a similar situation, but didn't have a good outcome. I'm reminded of those who struggle with a situation that I can't imagine going through. To those people I would just like to say, "May God bless you."

May God bless you when you struggle. May He bless you when you are strong and when you are weak. May He bless you when you need him the most, when you don't feel like you can go on, or when you feel like you can do it on your own. In all things you do, may He bless you.

4

ood friends are hard to come by, but if we are lucky
we find one or two who will stick by us no matter
what. I've had many good friends throughout my life
but most end up more like acquaintances over time. I
have learned over the years that I am not good at keeping
close friends. Sometimes I tell myself it's because people
don't really understand me, which makes it hard to maintain a friendship. Other times I tell myself it's because I
don't really want people to know too much about me. But
perhaps the truth is that I really don't converse very well,
so most of the time I come off as a jerk.

I have never been good at communicating and it
has worked well for me that people know me as shy or
just being quiet. Having this reputation has allowed me
to not have to express myself at all. The downside to

this is now I can't express myself at all. But whether this is a symptom or the prognosis, this may very well be one thing that stops me from having any long-lasting friendships. It hasn't kept me from meeting some amazing people, though.

Church and the fire service have an amazing way of producing some of the most sincere people anyone could ever meet. They also generate an assortment of people with a vast set of skills. People often show off their talents in order to benefit those who matter to them. I find it reassuring to find someone who is willing to put whatever they are doing aside in order to help out a friend in need. There is a spot in our hearts reserved for friends who put our well-being ahead of theirs. These are the friends I find myself drawn to; not because I want them to do things for me, but because these are the people I want to imitate.

Ben is one of those annoying people who is good at everything. He will also drop what he is doing to help a friend. Ben started on the fire department as a volunteer a couple years after I did. I was one of the drill instructors for the fire academy and would call out the cadences as we ran in formation. Ben had a case of what he referred to as exercise-induced bulimia. Every Saturday morning as we went on our run, he would excuse himself from the group, find the nearest shrubbery, and vomit. As a group, we would circle around to pick him up, and he would hop back in formation and continue the run.

The next year I came up with an ominous cadence inspired by Ben. It referred to a recruit who started off not doing so well, but continued to push himself. The cadence concludes with this person becoming "The best Chief in the USA." Although he is not a Chief yet, I think it speaks for how much he has pushed himself. He was hired by a neighboring fire department not long after he started as a volunteer. And now we get to see pictures of him with his goofy grin as he and his crew head out of state on deployment to fight yet another wildfire.

When we bought our first house, Molly and I had the great idea to move in on New Year's Day. Because of this, not many people were willing to lend a hand, so we were already short-handed. Moving day came, and we had a couple people call to let us know they couldn't make it. We ran through the list of people who may be around and willing to help. First on the list was Ben. He reassured us he would be right over and asked who was there to help. We gave him the list of people but he didn't find the small quantity of individuals to be acceptable. He assured us he would be recruiting more friends. So Ben being Ben, he called a couple of fellow firefighters he knew would be around, and suddenly we had three more sets of able arms to carry heavy furniture. Thank you Ben!

Like moving on a holiday, Molly and I have some-how managed to find the more difficult ways of getting things done. We also have a knack for owning cars that break down at the most inconvenient time. Not that there is a really good time, but Interstate 80 in the middle of nowhere Nebraska or a dirt road in southern Colorado would probably top my list of places I would prefer not to have my car suddenly stop working. And of course it always has to be a weekend, so any repair shop won't even be able to look at the car for a couple days, at which point they will of course explain how they don't have the necessary part in stock and it will take a week for delivery.

We probably wouldn't have so many issues if we'd keep up with vehicle maintenance, but without any money to spare, we sometimes push off auto repairs until absolutely necessary. Clunking and grinding from the front axle should meet the criteria as being absolutely necessary.

I finally had a more convenient time for my car to break, as I was driving home one day and heard a snap from the front of the car. Of course I felt the urgency to complete the necessary repairs. I was sure the car wouldn't drive any further, and since I was only a mile from home, I figured I would coast as far as I could and then push the car the rest of the way. I pressed the accelerator and somehow the car managed to propel forward, so I continued home.

When I started to hear the ominous sounds of failing parts coming from the front of my car, I asked Ben if he knew how to replace a CV joint. He had previously told me he made the same repairs on another firefighter's car, so I kept this in the back of my mind, knowing this repair would need to happen soon. When I heard the snap, I immediately thought to call Ben.

"Hey dude. I think the CV joint on my car finally went out. Do you think you could give me a hand?" I hate asking for help, but since he had already offered, and I thought it would be more insulting to not seek his help after the offer, I felt I was in the clear.

Ben was quick to help. "Do you think you can make it here?"

"I don't think so. I'm surprised I was able to make it home."

Ben lived about fifteen miles away so I didn't want to take the chance of getting stuck in the middle of the road, halfway there. He let me know he would have to grab his flatbed trailer and then he would be over. He pulled up in front of the house and I attempted to drive my car up the ramp onto his trailer. I made it about five feet and the front axle snapped completely through. Okay, this was going to be a little more difficult now. The plan was to push the car as best as we could and see how far it could make it up the ramp. Once the car ceased to accelerate up the ramp, I would pull the emergency break. I suppose most stories would have some hilarious explanation of what events resulted from attempting this feat, and because that's the way things seem to go in my life, one would expect nothing less, but it worked.

My car came to rest halfway up the ramp. Ben secured his chain to the front of my car and started using the hand winch to pull the car the rest of the way. And then the winch broke. There it was; I should have known it wasn't going to be that simple. We then strapped a couple ratchet straps to the front of the trailer and secured them to the front of my car. We used the straps to slowly ratchet the car onto the trailer. It wasn't the easiest way of getting the job done, but my car was soon on the trailer, and off we went. Thanks again, Ben!

It seems to me that everybody knows someone we look at and wonder how they get so much done in the time they have to do it. They always seem busy, but then they always have time for you. I think Brian must sleep about an hour a day. He started as a volunteer on the fire department the same time Ben did. As a volunteer I worked twelve-hour shifts on weekend nights, and Brian joined my crew soon after he started. When we got to the station, we would eat dinner, get some things done around the station, and then most of us would head to bed. And as it always seemed to be on weekends, we would get a call about one or two o'clock in the morning, and Brian would still be up working on something.

It was usually his truck or somebody else's vehicle that he had pulled into an open bay.

Soon after my wife and I got married, Brian helped me get a job at the Urgent Care where he worked and trained me during my instructional period. He loved to point out that I was the new guy since I had more seniority than he did on the fire department. But soon he left the Urgent Care to work as a tech at a nearby hospital. We continued to work weekends at the fire station together, and he would do the shopping for dinner for the crew. Brian prided himself in his frugality and boasted that he could get dinner for the entire crew for the cost of a postage stamp. He was always keeping himself busy, and if he wasn't working, volunteering, snowboarding, or mountain biking, he was usually helping someone else fix up their car or lawnmower or something.

Brian was the guy who was never going to get married or have kids. He was too busy with life. Religious would have been one of the last words I used to describe him, but our conversations never went that direction. He knew I attended church and I knew he was Jewish, but that was the extent of our religious knowledge of each other. One typical morning, we were getting off shift and heading to our cars. We started chatting and Brian told me about a woman he worked with—Grace—who invited him to church with her. Grace explained to him that she sang at her church and asked him to join her. Brian was excited as he explained how he was expecting her to be part of a choir, but was shocked that she was one of a couple singers in the small church band. He told me how the pastor at her church was so relatable, and was even talking about mountain biking. Brian was intrigued.

Like every other aspect of his life, Brian was all in with his new church. He was excited. Brian was truly a man of God. He continued to be the same man he was, but with a new purpose. He helped others. He spoke about God. And he got married. My wife and I continued to have kids, ending up with three, and Brian and Grace had a couple boys. Some say people change after they get married and have kids. They don't make time for their friends like they did before. I think maybe Brian found a way to create time.

Molly and Grace got along great from the beginning. I couldn't tell Brian about any car problems I had without him demanding I bring the family and the car to his house. Grace would make dinner, she and Molly would hang out with the kids, and Brian and I would work on the cars in his driveway with Christian music playing in the background. When dinner was ready, we would open a beer and head inside to wash up.

Brian taught me what it meant to do things for other people. In our neighborhood at that time, everyone had juniper bushes in their front yards. We decided to take them out at basically the same time, and Brian was right there to help. Our neighbors to the east bought their house after it went into foreclosure, and it was greatly in need of repair. One issue was the half-dead cotton-wood tree in the front yard. Our neighbor trimmed the branches in order to keep them from falling onto the house, but he would need assistance taking down the rest of the tree. Enter Brian.

The plan was to take the tree down in thirds. We began with the top third, as one would expect. We secured a ladder, and Brian ascended the tree and made the necessary relief cuts. We tied one end of a rope to the top of the tree and the other to Brian's truck. The plan was to keep tension on the rope and pull the top of the tree away from the house. After the relief cuts were made, we wanted to see if they were adequate, so Brian hopped in his truck and began to pull.

At this point we had gathered an audience of curious neighbors, each equipped with a cell phone set to record a video of what was about to happen. As Brian started pulling, the entire tree began to lean from the bottom so he stopped. The tree then began to swing in the direction of the house.

"Keep going! Keep going!" I frantically motioned to Brian and he pressed the accelerator, uprooting the entire tree. The fifty-foot tree came down across the yard, across the driveway, missed the basketball hoop, and ended in the street. Perfect placement. It wasn't the way we planned, but it worked out. The spectators erupted in applause.

Brian then pulled out a chainsaw and gas-powered log splitter he'd borrowed from a family member, and we dismantled the tree. I collected the pieces and added them to my woodpile for our wood-burning fireplace as payment. Brian took nothing. When we were finished, he cleaned up the log splitter. He then told me something I will always hold onto. Whenever he borrows something, he makes sure to return it in better condition than when he got it, whether it's cleaning it up, sharpening a blade, or tuning up the engine. I was always taught that when you borrow something, return it the way you got it. But Brian wanted to give more than he received.

We don't get together with Brian and Grace as often as I would like to. And I will never be able to repay him for the things he has done for me. But just like when he refused to let me pay him back when we had to borrow money, I will have to do what he requested then: Pay it forward.

When our youngest child was born I had been a career firefighter for almost two years. When she was about four months old, I picked up a shift at the fire station, which put me on for three days straight. Four hours into my third day I got a frantic phone call from Molly who was obviously in distress. "Our house is on fire!"

That's not one of the things you expect when you are working a shift at the fire station, so I was caught off guard. I wasn't really sure what that meant. Was it like the time I let bacon drippings gather on the bottom of the oven, causing a fire in the contained box where it belongs? She was a little frantic about that one as well.

"Do I need to come home?" Maybe I should have thought of a better question in order to determine the severity of the situation.

"Yes!" She wasn't joking around.

I hurried into the Battalion Chief's office, briefly explained the situation, and explained that I needed to leave. He was very understanding and told me not to worry about anything there; they would get my spot covered. I probably would have left anyway.

As I was driving home as quickly as I could, making sure to obey all traffic laws, Molly called again to see how far away I was. "They are cutting a hole in our roof!" Okay, this was a little bigger than I originally thought.

When I arrived at home, the fire crews were wrapping up everything. The Battalion Chief explained what they had done, and the Captain on the first-due engine brought me inside and showed me the damage as he began to investigate what started the fire, which turned out to be an electrical malfunction in the dryer. Our laundry room was in the bathroom upstairs, and as we headed that direction I realized the damage wasn't as bad as I expected.

Molly had closed the door to the bathroom as she was exiting the house with the three kids, and the fire was contained to the upstairs bathroom. The rest of the house only had smoke and water damage, albeit quite a bit of damage. In the fire department, we do extensive training on how fire and smoke move throughout a building, and we emphasize the need for closing doors. Some departments, in fact, designate someone in charge of door control. During public education events we explain how closing bedroom doors can save lives. I saw evidence of this play out in my own house.

Not long after the fire crews left, friends started showing up. Guys from my shift stopped by to offer anything they could. At the time I was assigned to the ambulance, and my partner was the first person to show up. Not long after he arrived, he left our house to grab us some lunch because he knew that was the last thing we would be thinking about. After a week or so living in a hotel, we were invited to his house for dinner with he and his wife.

Josh was a volunteer Battalion Chief on our department, and a career Lieutenant for a department farther south. As we looked around our house trying to accept the reality of what had happened, he showed up with his family, his support, and a check from his career department to help out with whatever we needed. As we walked through the house, we continued to point out our amazement at the amount of damage in the bathroom, and how much the flimsy bathroom door contained the fire to that room.

We find out who our true friends are when we are struck with tragedy. But in tragedy we can also acquire new friends. Donnie had been a longtime volunteer on our department, but retired before I started. He was elected to our Board of Directors just prior to the fire in our home. Donnie had been physically disfigured from multiple surgeries after suffering from skin cancer, but never let it get the best of him. Other than this, I knew nothing about him save some stories I'd heard from members who worked with him. I think my favorite recollection is them reminiscing about his specific way of pumping. Our training to drive and operate the engines includes extensive training on how to calculate proper pump pressures. This allows the correct flow of water, and allows the firefighters on the nozzle to be able to manage the hose. Donnie's philosophy was to throttle up until the pressure was enough to start to lift the firefighters off the ground, and then back off just a little.

I got a glimpse of Donnie's heart shortly after our fire, when I got a letter from him containing a personal check in my mailbox at the fire station. I was unaware, but he previously had an idea of starting a fund for residents of our district who suffered from a fire. Shortly after our incident I got an email with a brief description of the fund he was looking to start, and a request for anyone interested to contact him. I jumped at the opportunity. We soon developed our fire victims fund, and I learned more about the compassion Donnie had for others than I would ever have imagined.

I would have been happy to call Donnie a friend and hope he would have referred to me as such. That winter I got an email from our Fire Chief addressed to the department advising us that Donnie passed away while he was shoveling snow. I sat at the kitchen table as I read the email, and was unaware of my surroundings until I heard my older daughter ask, "Mommy, why is Daddy crying?" I tried to keep my composure as I explained to her that a friend of mine from the fire department had just died. I just wish I'd gotten to know him better than I did.

If we are lucky, we find a friend who will stick by us our entire lives. And some friends may only be there for a short time. But if they are true friends, they will change our lives forever. Some of the people I have had the pleasure of knowing have taught me what it means to really care about others. And if these are some of the people I can try to imitate, maybe I can pay it forward and leave a lasting impression on someone looking for a friend.

5

"You sound like my grandpa when you puff like that." Molly usually catches on to the subtleties of my increased stress levels before I do. One of my stress habits is slowly exhaling through pursed lips. I'm not quite sure why I do this. I'm sure it's the same as everything else; it started off simple and became complex over time. I can't wait to see what it turns into. It could be a subconscious way of lowering my blood pressure by stimulating the vagus nerve (look it up, it's a thing), or it could just be habitual. I should be careful because it could also cause me to pass out. I tend to have low blood pressure anyway, so I don't think dropping my blood pressure is extremely necessary. Maybe I'm just regulating my oxygen and carbon dioxide levels. But I'm not a doctor so I won't pretend to be. But for some reason or another, breathing like this just makes me feel better. And I find that, more often than not, I do this while I'm driving.

I enjoy living close to and being in the mountains. It's driving behind all of the out-of-staters and transplants who refuse to use the slow vehicle pull-offs that is less than desirable. My wife offers to take on the burden, but I insist on driving. Each time she reminds me of her proposition to give me a sedative and let her drive. I pretend to not be intrigued by the idea but secretly I think it would probably be a good decision.

From our house we take the back roads through alpaca farms and past enormous houses, on even more massive properties, perched high enough on the foothills to overlook the Front Range. We point out all the horses to our youngest daughter, and hope to see an elk or a couple deer as we make our way to Highway 34. We meet the highway at the base of the Big Thompson Canyon, and make our way up the winding road.

We proceed through the last turn and are reassured that we are in Estes Park when we see the street sign for Mall Road. We descend slightly into town and are suddenly surrounded by the peaks of the Rocky Mountains. The Stanley Hotel sits on the hill to the north. Also to our right are the Twin Owls, an amazing rock formation appropriately named due to the striking resemblance to two owls nuzzling to keep warm throughout the chilling

Rocky Mountain winter. We feel at home here. I have never lived too far away, but recently we moved only a couple miles from where the Big Thompson River flows from Estes Park and exits the Big Thompson Canyon. It now feels more like home than before.

Now we sit in traffic where Highway 34 and Highway 36 meet, as locals and tourists converge on Elkhorn Avenue, the main stretch through town. Locally-owned shops line the road as tourists flock to the streets with ice cream cones in hand, no matter the season. We fight our way through the sea of oversized motorhomes, rental cars, and all the other vehicles with out-of-state plates, counting the alternate routes we could've taken to bypass the downtown area. But for some reason there is comfort in watching people from all over the world enjoy the area we call home, knowing they will leave with fond memories of their once-in-a-lifetime vacation. I remind myself of this feeling when we are on vacation and we become the tourists. It seems to help the anxiety, temporarily at least, when I internally reverse the roles.

We make our left turn toward Rocky Mountain National Park, which we refer to as "the park," leaving our children wondering why there is no playground equipment. And we point out the vehicles whose drivers are obviously trying to decide which way they need to go. As we creep along with traffic, we watch the tourists patiently waiting to take their photos in front of the sign for Rocky Mountain National Park.

Park Rangers sit inside their five-square-foot cabins and stop vehicles filtering into the park as if they are the gatekeepers of the mountains. After paying their entrance fee, visitors are given a map of the park and sent on their way. As we approach this convergence of vehicles, we are always amazed at the constant flow of traffic. With an undeserved, elevated sense of self-worth, we stay to the right and pull into the lane meant only for those with a pass. We pull up to the gate, and I clutch onto our card as if someone will jump out from behind the post and snatch it. I swipe the card and the gate is lifted from our path. We pass by all the other vehicles that were recently in front of us and continue on as if we had been given backstage passes to the concert of the year.

Ego meets reality when we find ourselves at the back of the line of cars; the passengers contained within are hoping to catch their first glimpse of a herd of elk. Now we have to wait in traffic again until we are able to reach the parking lot of whichever adventure we choose on this particular day. I catch myself puffing again.

Stress in a given situation is relieved when the circumstances change. The situational anxiety caused by driving is relieved soon after reaching my destination. It is predictable and avoidable. I know when I drive down the interstate or through the mountains that I will be stressed by the traffic. If I want to avoid this stress, I don't drive. I want to take my family hiking. I want to sit on top of a boulder overlooking an elk herd. So I subject myself to the frustrations of necessary transportation.

True anxiety has many faces. From a lifetime of staring into the cold, lifeless eyes of each, I have memorized every curve, every freckle, every contour. Which face I see determines how I will attempt to combat the onslaught of torment it brings with it. For one face, I seek the reassurance of friends or family. For another face, I seek out cool air. For yet another, quiet solitude. But as I attempt to defend myself, I know I am without a sufficient counter attack. I am only able to hold my defense until time rescues me from the agony. The enemy attacks with the faces of anxiety, and with each attack I draw from my belt the only weapon I possess to combat it—perseverance.

Sweat beads on my forehead and under my eyes. I feel my body temperature rise, yet my extremities are cold. Like condensation rolling down a glass of ice water in the summer, I feel a drip of sweat running down my spine. I despise this face. He comes from nowhere and is summoned by the slightest thought of the alteration of normalcy. For some reason he tends to come around while I am shaving. And since I use an electric razor, the sweat that accumulates on my face makes the act of shaving more difficult, thus adding to the anxiety.

Anxiety is a bitterly cold snowball tumbling down the unforgiving Rocky Mountains. Calming reassurance acts as a tree to break it apart. But anxiety let loose can snowball into an avalanche big enough to destroy the most massive trees in its path. This face of anxiety develops rapidly and any attempt to halt snowball formation only causes accelerated growth. The more I try to not think about this face causes me to think about how I am trying not to think about it. And thinking about not thinking about it, paradoxically, is thinking about it. The face looks at me and laughs.

Faith is tested when a plea for help is not answered to our liking. This face stares me in the eye as I look toward Heaven requesting peace. The sweat continues to pour. Deep breath is followed by deep breath in my attempt to fight off yet another attack. With each exhalation my lips whisper a faint "Please help." The face forces itself into my field of vision and tells me that if I truly had faith I could succeed in warding off this attack. I start to believe this to be true. Now I begin to ask for the faith needed to fight off the attack. Another bead of sweat drips down my back.

I ask for relief from my symptoms, but things just get worse. I tell God that if He doesn't miraculously cure my pain, I won't do what I believe in my heart He wants me to, as though I can bribe Him. But my pain continues to get worse, and I continue to rebel. I argue and attempt to persuade God to heal me, but no relief is found. Then my heart tells me to act against the promise of my words, and I begin to write some more.

It is true that actions speak louder than words, and my heart is more sincere than my mouth. I only hope God sees the willingness of my heart and not the slander of my words.

As thoughts race, a new face of anxiety appears. He thrives on noise and chaos. He causes a sense of worry and worthlessness. He tells me that the rest of the world holds me in judgment, and nothing I do is ever good enough. I begin to feel as though the world is closing in on me. Every voice and every sound is exaggerated until everything becomes one loud roar, and eventually I don't feel like I can deal with another second. With him comes an overwhelming urge to scream as loud as I can. My hands start shaking and my heart starts racing. I feel the need to crawl out of my skin or run straight through a wall.

My children beg and plead for us to take them somewhere fun. I push it off as long as I can because I know what comes with it. Molly takes the children's side, and off we go. I watch them have fun, and my heart is happy. I even begin to play with them. But in the blink of an eye my contentment vanishes and anxiety sets in. Too much noise, too many questions, another child coughing where my children are playing, someone cutting in front of my children in line, someone speaking impolitely, or whatever the case may be, can cause this face to stare me down, letting me know he's been standing right next to me this entire time. If I had any hair, I would pull it out. I hate this face with all of my being.

When I was younger he only came around with unexpected circumstances beyond my control. Now he never leaves. His voice echoes in my brain. Sometimes I hear him as a whisper; other times he shouts loud enough to be heard over the joyful laughter of my children. This face has built the foundation of anger within me.

With each passing day this voice becomes louder. I make a feeble attempt to drown it out, but he just won't shut up. He is that annoying person who thinks you want to hear his opinion on every subject. I just don't want to hear about it unless it's important. Maybe that's why he keeps getting louder. He must be a narcissist.

My oldest child's favorite ride at Elitch Gardens in Denver is the Tower of Doom. It's a cylindrical tower with three open-air pods surrounding the perimeter. You start off this ride by getting buckled into what feels like a toddler's car seat, with your back toward the tower alongside three other helpless individuals. The other two pods contain like-minded individuals who think perhaps this could be fun. The thickly padded shoulder harness drops over your head and is buckled into the seatbelt-style buckle between your legs, and since everyone in the pod is facing the same direction, you can't see the look of terror on the faces of your ill-fated friends. The line of thrill-seekers encircles the tower, so that no matter what direction you face, you can warn those who will soon share in your terror that they can still back out, even though it is too late for you. And for some reason or another, there is always at least one pod that isn't running. Throughout my multiple trips, I've been told by the staff the reason for this is anything from the wind being too strong, to maintenance, to "It got stuck." This makes me feel better. And I keep going back.

Once everyone is buckled, you gaze upon the two high-schoolers whose job it is (their first job, by the way) to control your fate with the push of a button. They both give a thumbs up and up you go. You ascend over two hundred feet and soon you can see all of Denver. At first you enjoy looking at all the sights. You can see where the Denver Broncos play, and no matter who owns the naming rights to the stadium, we Colorado natives will always refer to it as "Mile High." You see Coors Field and the oddly shaped "cash register" building that stands out from all the other skyscrapers.

At this point the amazement is wearing off and you begin to wonder how much longer this ride will be going up and at what point you will be coming down. It slows as it approaches the top, but it's deceiving because you think it will stop. It keeps going up. And then you hear the "thunk." You have reached the top. When you watch from the bottom, this momentary pause before you begin to descend is extremely brief. But they built the Tower of Doom to peak in the exact spot where time does not exist. It has physicists baffled to this day.

At the top there is a point between the time you hear the thunk of the ride resting at its apex and the time you are released. This is the time when anxiety is at its highest point. You begin to recount the decisions you have made up to this point and wonder if you have indeed righted all your wrongs. You are nervously sweating; your heart is racing. You can literally feel all of the tension in your body just before you are released to free fall as your stomach becomes wedged in your esophagus. From the bottom, all you hear is the woooosh. Not a scream is heard from any of the riders because it's physically impossible to scream with your stomach hanging out of your mouth and your lungs protruding from your nose like a pumpkin plant emerging from the ground.

The moment before the release from the top is how I feel every day. I live at the peak of the Tower of Doom. I am waiting to be dropped, and am wondering if the redundant brake system at the bottom will catch me as I descend, as it has for all those who have gone before, and I know will for all those who follow. That is now the anxiety in which I live.

I continue to wonder why God does not relieve my anxiety and my requests for help are left unanswered. I forget that each time I struggle, I continue to make it through. Is this God reaching into my life in order to control it? Or does He maintain his promise of free will, allowing me to maintain control, giving me the strength to persevere? I have seen how many times I have been caught at the bottom of my own Tower of Doom. But no matter how many times I am witness to my own life, I still feel that I am not in control and I begin to question God's sincerity. I recall all my trials and my continued struggle in daily life. I wonder why it is I can't be who I want to be. Why don't I have control over the thoughts in my own head? And if I feel that I cannot control my own life and can't trust that God truly cares for me, then do I conclude that I am really without faith?

As Christians, we don't accept a lie about our faith when it is obviously a lie. But if the lie is just a tweak of the truth, we accept it a little at a time until the full lie is now our perception of the truth. Evil attempts to convince me that if I truly had faith I could control the actions of God and God would alter reality for my benefit. If I believe this, I am left to assume that my failure is a result of God's lack of compassion.

My failure to recognize God's compassion does not mean that he is without it. It may just be that I am not capable of understanding the deepest thoughts of the Creator of all that is. But I wonder why I am left without explanation of why things are the way they are. If I think I should be able to control God just because I have faith, am I the narcissist?

6

The world does not have a shortage of pet peeves or people who love to point theirs out to anyone willing to listen. Each of us has something in particular that annoys us—something that makes our skin crawl no matter who does or says such ridiculousness. I know many people who could write a book solely about their pet peeves.

I'm not sure if I could classify it as a pet peeve, but one thing I find particularly obnoxious is the improper use of terminology, specifically when people misdiagnose themselves to appear worse off than they are. I have been guilty of this, so I do see the irony. Sometimes people just want attention, but more often than not, they just don't know what they are talking about. And I don't exclude myself from this. People hear a term used out of context, so they in turn use it out of context in a later setting. This perpetuates until the real meaning of the word has long since been forgotten.

I often hear people explain how they had the "flu," referring to either a stomach bug or a general upper respiratory infection. Sometimes I let it go, and other times I begin the inquisition until I get enough information to correct their mistake. Most of the time it's the former; I'm not a doctor, after all. The flu, or influenza, is a specific virus that has who knows how many strands and causes upper respiratory symptoms. I won't go into detail about it because I would even bore myself trying to write about it. However it has lead to many people wondering why they still got a cold or a stomach bug even though they received their flu shot. Instead of educating people on the fallacy of their incorrect self-diagnosis, we let it go; and now people are left explaining how they had the flu when in reality they just had more drastic symptoms of an ordinary virus than what they are used to.

I spent several years working at an Urgent Care, working my way to become the clinic manager, while I awaited my much anticipated firefighting career. Each patient would fill out their intake form, and, depending on the reason for their visit, we grabbed the appropriate exam form before we called them back to triage. Many times people would write down their symptoms such as "cough" or "knee pain." Other times they would diag-nose themselves by writing "the flu" or "broken ankle." When we had a form that indicated the person thought they had the flu, we grabbed the upper respiratory ill-ness form. We filled in their name, date of birth, and whatever we could before calling them back. Once in triage, we asked their symptoms, and for some reason we were shocked each time they described how they were unable to stop vomiting for the past several days. Now we had to grab another form and start over. I'm sure the patients weren't too happy having to wait while holding their vomit bucket.

I think pet peeves must be contagious, though, because I seem to have picked one up from my wife. This is the improper use of "migraine" to describe a headache. This is one I have been guilty of in the past until Molly showed me the error of my ways. Just don't tell her I admitted that I was wrong.

I have been a firefighter almost half my life. I have seen many people suffering from various severities of pain, so I am very skeptical when someone tells me their "migraine" is a nine out of ten on the pain scale when they are fully functioning and show no outward distress. I have no doubt these people are in pain, and I am fortunate enough to never have experienced a true migraine. However, I have witnessed many people, my wife included, completely incapacitated while suffering from a true migraine. I have no desire to know what that feels like. So unless I am curled up in a ball hugging my knees, the minor ache I have in my head is manageable, and I have no business complaining about it, at least not all day.

I don't intend to describe proper medical terminology because I want to cease the incorrect use of the term "the flu" or "migraine." Well, maybe a little. I want to make a point that when we use a term to describe something it's not, we do it a disservice. This is how we are left explaining how someone sneezing so hard they hit their head on the table is awesome, leaving no adequate word to describe the sunset over the mountains when the moon and clouds are in just the right spot, or the feeling of holding your newborn child for the first time. And we are skeptical of those who explain how they suffer from an illness because the term for said illness has been overused.

This is why I think the one that bothers me the most is when people explain how their "OCD" won't let them complete a task or overlook something out of place. I have suffered from obsessive-compulsive disorder as long as I can remember. It is something I battle with, and at no point have I attempted to bring it to other people's attention when I am uneasy in a situation. Don't get me wrong, though. I'm not saying that nobody who has OCD has ever said anything about their OCD getting in the way. What bothers me is when people use "OCD" to describe themselves when they have a quirk. Plus, I would rather not bring it up and have to explain all my other behaviors, or even draw attention to it at all.

I stand by as people explain how they "had" to adjust the picture frame on the wall because it was askew and their OCD wouldn't let them leave it that way. I overlook another person's comment in a crowded room as they adjust the collar of a friend's shirt because their OCD won't allow them to let it go. I do this partly because I am passive and don't like confrontation, but mostly because if I explain what it really means to be obsessive-compulsive I may be called out and left to reveal my secrets. If that were the case, I know the face of anxiety would descend on me rapidly, followed by uncontrollable sweating.

The term "obsessive-compulsive" refers to repetitive thoughts and repetitive behavior. Not unlike anxiety and depression, this can be debilitating. Having to deal with this illness daily is frustrating for me, but I would still argue that mine is a mild form. My friends and coworkers joke about my incessant hand washing. I joke along with them. But it's not because I have the need to wash my hands as often and as long as I do that makes me obsessive-compulsive. It's because I'm obsessive-compulsive that makes me wash my hands as often and as long as I do. Being fearful of germs is only part of it. Plus, washing your hands often is just good practice.

"One, two, three, four, five, six, seven, eight, one, two, three, four, five, six, seven, eight…" and so on. This continues in my mind as I wash my hands. Each motion gets its own progressive number until I feel my hands are sufficiently clean. Stand by. I'm almost done. Trust me, it's as annoying for me as it is for those watching, if not more. I've suggested numerous times that the sinks I frequent should be equipped with a foot pedal. When I'm finally finished, of course, I must dry my hands. Here we go again. "One, two, three…" You get the picture.

The actions taken for someone with obsessive-compulsive disorder feel as necessary as breathing. Not completing the necessary deed is taking away a function required to stay alive. You suddenly experience overwhelming fear and you can't seem to catch your breath. Just the thought of failing to follow through with the task causes your heart to race. Once again you find yourself at the top of the Tower of Doom. Upon completion of your action, the button has been pressed, allowing you to descend back to Earth in order to step back in line and await your next turn. You find yourself getting buckled in as you approach your next scheduled behavior.

Getting ready for work in the morning has developed into a finely tuned ritual that is broken down by the minute. The order of my routine may not make sense, and there are many steps I take unnecessarily. I travel up and down the stairs more often than I need. What takes me three or four trips downstairs could be completed in two or even one. But I have developed it over many years. Each extra step I take comes with a memory of how it came to be. And each task must be completed the proper way. Heading upstairs requires me to turn out the kitchen light, take seven steps toward the stairs, and begin my ascent with my right foot. I still count it out, but I have it down so smooth I could do it all in my sleep.

I can't change the routine unless something beyond my control occurs. I just hope the kids all stay in bed or someone may throw off my routine. I did this one thing before I did that other thing once before, and now I have to do it that way each time. One time I did that thing before I did this thing and I caught a cold and I'm sure the two are related. Heaven forbid one of my children or my wife interrupts my stride because someone needs to use the restroom.

I know it is ridiculous to conclude that I got sick because I tied my shoes underhand instead of overhand, or my daughter wanted to give me one more hug on her way back to bed, but that's how this illness works.

No matter how many times I tell myself that what I am doing doesn't make sense, I can't stop. I explain to myself each morning that I can gather my belongings from upstairs on the same trip I tell my sleeping family goodbye and remind them I love them. But if anything happened to my family, I know it would be because I altered the routine, and I couldn't imagine how I would feel knowing I caused anything bad to happen to any one of them. Whether it's one of them getting sick, or something worse.

We go many places as a family, and when we leave the house they know they have to head to the car first, and I will meet them there. I know the back door is locked. I know the garbage is put away so the dog doesn't get into it. But as soon as everyone is out of the house, I have to triple check that the garbage is put away, check the back door four times, and pass counterclockwise around the kitchen table on my way to the door. I then must lock the door handle, tell the dog goodbye just the right way (the increment of four depends on if the dog gets up to walk me to the door or if he stays put), close the front door, check the handle, lock the deadbolt, and then turn the key one more time to verify the deadbolt is locked.

This routine is harmless by itself. It's an example of one of the more understandable rituals I have to perform. I deal with it as something that doesn't take much time and is relatively stress-free. Like my other rituals, the problem isn't that I do it. The problem comes when something hinders me from carrying out my mission—when an audible is called and it alters the path I have set myself on. There is no reason that one of my children wanting to hold the door open for me should cause anxiety. But I have my assignment and there is no altering the plan.

The quarterback inside my brain has called out the play in the huddle. The defense shows a formation the quarterback was not expecting, so he calls an audible at the line of scrimmage. Because the linemen are unfamiliar with the defensive formation, they are unsure what their assignment is, and frustration and anxiety ensue. I should probably learn when to call a timeout.

One theory is that obsessive-compulsive disorder begins with one's inability to accept a loss of control over a certain situation. I may not be able to control whether I or someone in my family gets sick. There are countless circumstances that are beyond my control. The question is: Does God control my life, or does He leave it up to my own free will? Does my faith, or lack thereof, cause God to interfere with acts of nature in order for me to not be susceptible to one disease or another? Why do I think I'm so special?

I believe God knows the outcome of our actions, whether it saddens Him or brings Him joy, but He does not interfere with the laws of nature he created because that is what we demand of him. I have contemplated this a lot lately. Based on my observations and understanding throughout my life, I believe God has created all that we see and do not see by creating scientific laws of nature that even He must follow. This may not be a popular conclusion, or even correct, but to me this explains many of the questions I have asked, and the things I have witnessed. After all, how can the Creator of the universe make laws that do not pertain to Him? Then we would not really be created in His image. Due to this, we are susceptible to our own actions and those of others and of this world. Therefore, how could I expect that something like checking the light switch four times would change the outcome of an unrelated scenario?

But instead of trusting that God is God and has ultimate authority, and accepting that I am not in control of His actions, I have developed habits I can control. I conclude that if I can't overcome my own behavior and trust in God, I must not have faith. Or that if I even had faith as small as a mustard seed, I could move the mountains, or at least keep anything bad from happening to my family. I reintroduce myself to the conclusion of an alternative reality causing me to feel that nothing I ever do will be good enough. The reality is that I'm not good enough and never will be, but I don't have to be. But the face of anxiety shows up and tells me I have failed. I have failed myself. I have failed my family. I have failed God. Nothing I ever do will be good enough, and I can't even trust in the will of God. But my ability to maintain my faith when circumstances are beyond my control doesn't overpower the predetermined will of God.

Faith doesn't come from my ability to resist checking the light switch the correct number of times before I go to bed, or making sure I shave after brushing my teeth but before using mouthwash. Whatever alternative I find for an obsessive-compulsive behavior will only take the place of the previous behavior. I find my faith with the ability to alter my routine when everything inside is telling me that I have to push the lock button on the car door one more time, but instead I resist and assure myself that I am not in control. I find faith when I accept that what I want isn't necessarily how life will work out. If I can overcome the unbearable urge to follow through with an obsessive-compulsive behavior from time to time, maybe this is my way of telling the face of anxiety that he has no control over me. He tells me that I must complete my action, otherwise I am not in control. I look him in the eye, resist the presumably inevitable action, and assure myself that God is in control. Perhaps that is the kind of faith that is as large as a mustard seed.

7

One of the signs of depression is a lack of joy in activities that were once enjoyable. The problem is, when you have suffered from depression your entire life, these activities often don't exist. There are only events that cause a brief pause in the perpetual downward spiral, that in the blink of an eye give a glimpse of what it would be like to be happy.

There is a theory that everyone has a baseline level of happiness. If an event happens in someone's life that causes an increase in their mood, this will only be for a brief amount of time and they will revert back to their baseline. The reverse is true if something happens to make someone feel sadness. With depression, since the baseline is below that of the average person, when someone has an elevation in their mood and then gets knocked down, the fall is more drastic.

I have developed a fear of allowing myself to feel excitement. Each moment of anticipation is met suddenly by the negativity of disappointment. When you spend your time at the bottom, you begin to get hopeful when you see a way to the top. As you approach the summit, you feel that maybe you can join everyone else as they enjoy the view, and you can share the same feelings they possess. With depression you are left with few handholds and footholds. The slightest jostle can cause you to fall. From the top, the smallest mistaken look or misinterpreted statement from anyone can cause you to plummet.

The joy of watching your children play basketball can be ruined by the misconception that your spouse is asking you to scoot over because they can't stand touching you anymore when in reality they continue to get elbowed by the person on the other side. Despite your spouse explaining this during or after the game, you are now at the bottom and no explanation can provide enough leverage to pick you up onto your feet, let alone lift you back to the top.

Throughout my life I have learned to not allow myself to feel any sense of happiness. This is the result of a series of events that to other people may not be a big deal, but nobody else will understand how it has affected me. There is no way to really know how someone else truly feels. What is a big deal to one person may seem ridiculous to another. My scars run deep and each one brings a memory of how it got there.

For some reason I often find myself in a competition with people to see whose physical scars are worse. I start by displaying the smaller scars. I show off the scars on my fingers where I cut them on a bottle cap attempting to open a cola bottle for my wife when she had a migraine. We sat in the car after leaving the emergency room and I found myself sans bottle opener. She was pregnant with our third child and I was going to be the hero. I had the brilliant idea to open it with my pocket knife. Not the handy bottle opener supplied by a Swiss Army knife, but a single-blade pocket knife. My idea turned out to not be such a wise choice. I was left with a series of three scars across each of the four fingers on my right hand, as though I was in a battle with a miniature version of Wolverine from the X-Men.

From there I move on to the two small scars on my left forearm that each look like a half-moon. These were from when I was in elementary school and one of the girls down the street found it funny to dig her fingernails into my arm and pull out a chunk of skin. In the same area I show a short, narrow scar from my friend's facemask when he tackled me during football practice. I show my mangled fingernail on the ring finger of my right hand that never grew back properly after it got slammed in a door, and a round scar on my upper back from when I had the chickenpox.

I show the scars on my knees and elbows from what seemed to be a continuous open wound throughout school, caused by football and skateboarding. And I finish with the three-inch scar on my left flank. The story on this changes, but it usually ends with me performing some sort of heroic rescue. The truth always comes out that I was trying to jump on my dad's back when I was a kid and slipped and fell onto the corner of a box fan. I didn't even get stitches.

None of the stories of my scars are very exciting. But they are my stories and each one comes with a memory. I like to show them off, but my mental scars I keep hidden. Like the stories behind my tangible scars, my emotional scars are nothing spectacular. Each has its own memory. Like the time my mom helped me make a flower out of fabric. My parents were still married so I wasn't any older than seven or eight. I don't remember actually making it, but I remember I was so excited to show it to my dad. When he came home from work I hid it behind my back with the same excitement a father would have presenting his kids with a new puppy.

"Guess what I have behind my back." I had been waiting all day to show him.

As I stood there, my brother passed by and said, "It's a flower."

I was completely heartbroken. This shouldn't be a big deal, and there is no reason I should remember or care many years later. But with depression, scars run deep. Unlike my external scars, they don't fade. Every experience that has brought me joy has been followed by extreme pain. If you fall every time you climb a mountain, you learn to stick to the foothills. So I learned to keep myself grounded. Metaphorically, though, I still enjoy the mountains.

A misconception about depression is that it is solely the result of a negative experience that causes the person to have a different perspective. This is no truer than saying someone suffers from diabetes because they ate a cookie. People can suffer from psychological "abnormalities" for various reasons. But like someone who suffers from hypothyroidism, something within me just doesn't work right. Whether it's due to not having enough serotonin, the right amount of receptors, or whatever the case may be doesn't matter. I'm not who I am because of what I have gone through. I am who I am because these are the cards I was dealt.

Depression is like falling into the deep end of a pool when you can't swim, and I have had the privilege of experiencing both. I remember sinking beneath the surface, looking up, wondering if this was the end. In a panic I found the strength and ability to heave my way to the surface long enough to belt out a garbled

"HELP!" and take one more breath before plunging below the surface again.

When you think you are drowning, seconds last forever, so I have no idea how long this continued. I remember repeating this event, each time with less hope someone would hear my plea for help. But I had gotten my brother's attention and he leapt into the water and pulled me to the side of the pool. I think that a lot of people need someone to jump in to help instead of reluctantly asking, "You good?" as they pass by without even waiting for the answer just so they can check their mental box that allows them to sleep better at night knowing they offered their assistance.

As I get older, though, I find that my tendency is to pull others down with me. I have less hope that someone will jump in to drag me to the side. There is an increased skepticism that people are more apt to watch me drown while I call for help than to jump in and risk damaging the cell phone in their pocket. I realize this is a bit cynical, and a little obscure, but this is the mentality I have adopted that has allowed me to get from one day to the next without having to count on anyone else, which would inevitably leave me disappointed.

Life is a fight to survive, and each day is a battle. A battle to overcome. A battle to persevere. Wars are won and lost on the battlefield. We hear these clichés all the time but we don't pause to think about what they mean.

Some days the enemy troops advance on us and we fear the battle is lost. We are left battered and bruised with only our will to survive. Hope brings us to a new dawn. We awake with our wounds from the previous day beginning to heal but our strength is still failing. Without faith we are without hope. It is a faith that we will overtake the enemy. A faith that we will rise up. A faith that even though we carry the scars from yesterday and face battles today, we will find a new strength. A strength that will allow us to overtake the enemy tomorrow.

There is another misconception that someone who suffers from depression is always sad. The truth is, we adapt to our surroundings. The time spent feeling melancholy is minimal compared to the continual torment we deal with. We put on happy faces but we're numb to the rubbish that's building up every day. We listen to the complaints of others without regard to how they are really affected. Nobody knows the torment we go through on a daily basis, and if they did they wouldn't be complaining about how the bagger at the grocery store was short-tempered when they asked if they wanted their cereal boxes in one bag or two.

Convincing ourselves that we have it harder than everyone else is morbidly reassuring. But even though I have the same illness as many others, I honestly have no idea how much they truly suffer. I hear stories of what other people go through, and I know what I go through, but I wouldn't change places with them. I suffer in my own silence, but I own it. It's mine. Life is an old beater car that nobody else wants. I take pride in what I've put into it, and I wouldn't sell it.

I am who I am because of how I was created, whether that was by God's design or because He allowed His laws to play out naturally, and I drew one of the short straws. But whatever the case, I am who I am. In my sorrow is where I am who I want to be. Sorrow is where I keep my love, my empathy, my compassion. In sorrow my soul weeps. It weeps for those who have gone before. It weeps for souls looking to find their way. It weeps for the world and the injustice found within it. Sorrow is where hope rebuilds, looking for ways to overcome.

The ugly side of depression is where I spend most of my time. Full of self-doubt, full of self-loathing. It is my curse. This is where life is left unspoken. This is where hope breaks down and anger is born. This is where my heart hurts. Not for the world, but for myself. The ugly side is where people give up on life. Where the hope built in sorrow is overshadowed by the lie that life has been defeated. The lie told to us by evil that we become convinced is true.

But the truth in sorrow is where I find that the lie of the ugly side has no place. In sorrow I find clarity. In sorrow I find truth. In my sorrow is where I find God. Sorrow is fragile. It fades like dust in the wind blown away by a single spoken word from the world beyond sorrow. I have joy in my sorrow. I despise my ugly side.

Sorrow is found in solitude. I keep my sorrow hidden out of fear of losing it. But slowly the ugly side consumes it. So I clutch it in my hand until my knuckles turn white. My sorrow is a gift given to me by God. Like the parable of the talents, I must not bury it. So in my sorrow I write. What has been given to me is not mine; therefore, I attempt to share it with the world. I share it in hope. I share it in faith. Faith that sorrow will be understood. Faith that others will own it as I try to own mine, before it is consumed by the ugly side. Faith that we will overcome. Faith that those beyond this curse and this gift will understand. Faith that in the end it will all be washed clean.

8

Time refines the memories of people who have passed away or are otherwise no longer in our lives. The byproduct of the purification process is determined by the memories we extract. We either choose to remember all the bad experiences we had, or we decide that the good memories carry more weight and we expel the bad experiences from the forefront of our minds. Like scars, those experiences will remain. But we can choose to look past them and only recall their existence when we look back in order to not repeat the same events in the future.

There is a quote by Otto von Bismarck I will always remember seeing on a poster hanging in my high school: "Only a fool learns from his own mistakes. The wise man learns from the mistakes of others." So we look past the negative memories of those we've lost only as a way to keep from repeating their mistakes. We don't let them be imprinted in our minds as the final memories of who they were.

I was in Oregon when my stepfather passed away. It wasn't unexpected when he finally succumbed to cancer, but we were all hoping for a miracle. I wasn't there. I should have been.

I took a few weeks to travel with my girlfriend at the time. We drove from Colorado to California, California to Oregon, Oregon to Washington, and then back to Oregon. Our last stop was visiting my grandparents in Oregon before heading back home to Colorado. My older brother called me while we were there to give me the bad news. We packed up the car and headed back the next morning. My girlfriend couldn't drive a manual transmission, so I drove more than eighteen hours to my mom's house, stopping for about an hour at a rest stop for a quick front-seat nap.

We endured a springtime snowstorm in Wyoming and finally made it back in time for the chaos of preparing for a funeral. My stepfather was a pastor, and I recalled him reading the poem, "Gone From My Sight," by Henry Van Dyke on at least one occasion. My little brother now read this at his father's funeral. Then we all sat in silence as they played "Thank You For Giving to the Lord" by Ray Boltz. Throughout the memorial, several people got up to speak and recall things they remembered about Earl. Each story told conjured up memories of our own.

Earl and I never got along. Our interactions were limited to necessity, despite my mom's attempts to unite her family. I acted up a lot, and made sure my opinion was known to all when I felt as though any injustice had been done. Earl was an old-school man from Iowa and I doubt he cared too much about the opinion of a brat. I tormented my little brother as often as I could, and I imagine Earl did not appreciate his son getting picked on just because he was the smallest.

The negative memories I have of him are now obsolete. What remain are stories of vacations, adventures, and life, both thought-provoking and humorous. Some of the humor was brought on by his own intention, mostly at his expense.

He was a large man and stood nearly a foot taller than my mom. It isn't that he was necessarily obese, just large. His voice was as big as he was, and every time I hear the lyrics, "Then sings my soul, my Savior God, to Thee," it is as though I can hear his voice booming along with the song from Heaven. He had a permanent tan between the bottom of his calves and just above his knees on his otherwise pale body because he insisted on wearing his socks pulled up as far as they could go, and he wouldn't wear shorts that had the nerve to touch his knee. Perhaps he would have pulled his socks up higher if any material known to man could expand to fit around his giant calves. As it was, when he removed the socks, covering ankles as white as the socks he just took off, what was left were lines that would remain for hours as his legs tried to regain their original form after being shoved into a tube never meant to contain an object so large. When he was alive, this annoyed me. Now I remember and smile.

Earl snored loud enough to cause construction workers to come over and ask us to keep down the noise because it was drowning out the sound of their jack-hammering. Many vacations consisted of camping in the popup, and we found it difficult to sleep with all the snoring. You may think that he would have stayed up later to allow everyone else to fall asleep out of decency, but Earl slept any chance he could. My mom and brothers and I were confined to the camper during a rainstorm, so we made the most of it by playing Trivial Pursuit. Earl fell asleep and, of course, began to snore. I took it upon myself to mock him by responding with a snore of my own. Each snore was reciprocated with another until the cycle was broken by Earl's response of, "I DON'T snore!"

My mockery was like a mountain lion stalking its prey. Instead of approaching what I thought was a lame deer, I was startled to find I had been stalking a grizzly.

It probably would've been wiser if I hadn't done that again. This is where my brothers would learn from my mistake.

Looking back now, I feel like Earl lived his life with the intention to make memories. Memories that now consist of vacations, Christmas decorations, Frostys from Wendy's or Blizzards from Dairy Queen, and those ridiculous line-ridden ankles.

On our drive to Mount Rushmore, we stopped to see goats by the side of the road. My instinct would have been to continue driving in order to get to our destination because the kids were driving me crazy and I was ready to get there already. That probably should have been Earl's instinct as well, with three boys in the back seat, one of which was me complaining that we could have been there already if only they'd made the road straight instead of winding through what they pretend in South Dakota are mountains. Earl chose to stop and watch the goats.

I can't recall which trip it was, perhaps the same stretch of road on the same trip, when we came across a herd of deer and again Earl stopped. But this time he evaluated the situation, remembered we had cheese-flavored crackers in the car, realized my little brother was at the appropriate height where the top of his head was face level with the deer, and used my brother's head as a platter to feed some very confused woodland creatures.

Here is where you learn from Earl: Please don't feed the wild animals!

If an event could create a good story, Earl took that option instead of the safer alternative. My mom often found herself questioning his decisions, and I'm pretty sure I heard her blood pressure rising on multiple occasions.

Each Christmas Earl competed with the rest of the neighborhood to win first place for the best Christmas decorations. He added something new each year, including hand-decorated angels and a nativity scene cut from plywood. He always found himself in second place.

Now I find that I sit by and watch as Molly decorates the house for Christmas. I recall the effort put into decorating our house when I was a child and hope to live up to the memory, but I find one excuse after another and am lucky to toss up a handful of lights to make at least the front of the house look a little festive.

We may not have gotten along, and I should probably have more negative memories than positive, but what I think of when I remember Earl is the vacations we took and the entertaining stories he lived to create. These should be the moments we live for. Not the struggles we deal with between good times.

Time shapes the memories of those no longer in our lives, but it can also bring people back together. It has the ability to sever what was once mended. Time heals and tears apart, it molds and destroys, it purifies and contaminates. We attempt to use time to our advantage, but in the end we relinquish control to it. Perhaps instead of hoping time will make things better, we should take advantage of the time we have.

My father and I have spent much of our lives in competition with each other. Many times we get along well; other times we don't. As difficult as it may be for me to admit that someone else can affect who I am, I have to say that many aspects of my life are a direct result of my relationship with my father. Memories I try to make with my children are reminiscent of the memories I have from my own childhood.

Instead of addressing my concerns, I silently hold onto memories of dissatisfaction about the way my father raised me. Now I hold myself accountable for disciplining my children the same way. I attempt to alter my actions as my father's voice and behaviors spill out of me. Another face looks at me and tells me I will never be good enough for my own children. But in my disappointment in the fact that I can't be a better father, I wonder why I expected perfection from my dad when I struggle to even consider myself to be a decent parent.

Instead of spending my efforts focusing on how I don't want to behave toward my children, I tell myself I should focus on how I want to raise them. If only I could be the father I want to be. I can take the memories I have from when I was a child and apply them to my own children. The memories I have of my dad coaching my soccer, baseball, and football teams. Memories of camping and fishing. Time spent with my children should not consist of only the awkward moments between times of discipline.

At our Christmas get-together this past year, the stragglers who were last to leave had the task of pulling questions about their childhood from a miniature Christmas tree. I picked the ribbon requesting that I find three words to describe the values we were taught from our childhood. I think my dad was as terrified as I was about what answer I may come up with. But I felt I had to answer sincerely. After a long time of deliberation, I came up with, "faith, family, and fun." I was surprised by my answer, much like my dad was.

These are the values I attempt to teach my children, and I felt all other values I could come up with would fit into one of these categories. My dad taught me what hard work really means, but I feel this can be about both faith and family. He was often not around because of work, including picking up an evening job to ensure we would have a good Christmas or enough money for our annual vacation. Each time I dig a trench in my yard to install a retaining wall, or dig a hole to plant more shrubbery, I recall my dad in his sleeveless shirt, wailing away at the dirt in our backyard as he prepared to install his retaining walls. He took breaks to drink his ice water as the condensation dripped down the outside of the glass. He ate a lunchmeat sandwich with mayonnaise, mustard, cheese, and a leaf of lettuce. On the side he had plain potato chips. I attempt to recreate this in myself as my children watch my efforts, but I don't care for mayonnaise or mustard on my sandwich. For some reason I find the face staring at me as I try my best to finish the morning's work before lunch. I trudge inside as I prepare to eat the lunch Molly has made for me. I can't even make my own lunch. The face smiles.

Vacations with my dad were filled with the disappointment that they weren't as perfect as the image he had in his mind. We kids couldn't have expected more. Trips to California were spent buried in the sunbaked sand. Afterward my dad would whip our sand-covered feet with our socks because that was the way he was taught to get the sand off as a child. Nothing says love like whacking your child's feet with sandpaper, but it worked. The remainder of the vacation was spent with my dad attempting to recreate his childhood and reminiscing about when he was a kid. Nothing could bring it back, and I think that made him sad. But what he didn't realize is that our own memories were being made.

My dad chose to drive at night so the five of us children and my stepmom could sleep in the car. I was the last to fall asleep and the first to wake. As we drove, I watched the stars between pairs of oncoming headlights. The faint sound of Foreigner or Paul Revere and the Raiders playing on the radio broke the silence of the night. It was dark and quiet. My heart was content. But as much as I liked the silence of the night, I enjoyed waking up to the sights of the back roads leading through wine country. Everything felt simple.

Like my father, I wish to recreate the memories for my own children, but I don't succeed. My wife plans the vacations that she never had as a child and I make a feeble attempt to implant my memories into our children. I get angry when my plans don't work out. I should hold onto Molly's understanding that these are new memories we create as a family. I'm not sure why I can't just enjoy the time we have. There's that face again.

The effort I put into what I do is directly related to my faith. I find it difficult to accomplish anything, but I continue to trek forward. I work hard at what I do because it's the right thing to do and I have faith that God has hope for who I will turn out to be. But I'm not sure I'm doing it right. I told myself I didn't want to sacrifice time with my family in order to work a little extra, but that was a fate I couldn't defend against.

About the time Molly and I were planning our wedding, we had six jobs between us. One of mine was volunteering for the fire department. After we got married, the number of cumulative jobs declined, and when our daughter was born I was back to two. We spent the first three years of our daughter's life having one day off together, every other week. When Molly returned to work, we saw each other in passing, and this continued until our son was born. We would often meet at her work to swap cars, with the oblivious child unknowingly swapping parents. We felt like divorced parents when we stopped halfway between home and the fire station so I could hand our daughter off to Molly in a parking lot because she was getting out of work later than planned.

When our son was born, the chaos didn't dwindle. I took about a week off work, but went right back to the hectic routine. Due to the fact that our son had an unbelievable attachment to Molly, and that I didn't see him very often, I felt like I was a distant relative asking to hold someone's baby when it's obvious neither the baby nor the mother wanted to oblige. I'm pretty sure every time I finally gave in to the wailing, and handed him back to my wife, he gave me a look as if he was telling me I was now the second favorite man in her life. The wailing was coming from our son, not Molly. I think.

By the time our youngest daughter was born, I was hoping things would be different. I was a full-time employee for the fire department, and maybe having the job I tried so hard for so long to get would allow me to be the father I always wanted to be. But time wasn't on my side. My life was now shaped by time and experiences that molded me into who I had become. Memories of who I was, and who I wanted to be, were shadowed by a life lived waiting for a tomorrow that I continued to hope would be just beyond the horizon.

We take our family vacations and I spend my time waiting for something better to happen next. We plan our vacations well in advance, and recently we drove from Colorado to Georgia, insisting on making the drive in two days. There was no time to stop along the way, so we found ourselves frustrated with the frequent requests for restroom breaks. At the end of day two, we were in the midst of a downpour as we entered Georgia. My recent attempt to repair our windshield wipers left the blades dropping too far below the windshield, and the rubber on the blades had started to peel away. That helps with the anxiety.

We found our way through the rain, but in the dark we were unable to see our surroundings, so we had to trust that we crossed over the necessary bridges to find our way to St. Simons Island. We were encouraged when we found the street leading to Molly's aunt and uncle's house and found relief when we confirmed it was in fact the correct house. The fact that I was on vacation with my family should have provided me with satisfaction. History knows that would not be the case.

We had stopped in Kentucky to fuel up along the way and Molly filled our empty water bottles from the soda machine inside the gas station. This prompted our daughter to inquire as to what was wrong with the water. We explained to her that she was used to the fresh water in Colorado, and the water there has seasoning!

Now we found ourselves out to lunch with Molly's aunt and uncle. They, along with the other locals, suggested we don't drink the tap water. We encouraged our children to drink lemon-lime soda, but our daughter wanted nothing of the sort. All the poor child wanted was a glass of water, so she insisted the server bring water. We ordered her the soda as a backup. This proved to be the proper decision, which was confirmed with the sour look on her face as our daughter choked down a mouthful of ocean-flavored water.

This was the first time I'd set eyes on the Atlantic Ocean and I was amazed at the warmth of the water in June. I looked on as our older daughter bodysurfed with Molly's uncle as the instructor. My five-year-old son was content sitting in the shallows and letting the trickling waves lift him slightly on his boogie board, just enough to move him a couple inches at a time before they retreated to the ocean. Molly and I took turns getting our cardio workout chasing our two-year-old daughter as she ran full speed toward the ocean, joyfully calling out, "Wawa!" We left the beach, and because I love my children, I whipped the sand off their feet with a sock. Tradition continues.

Prior to the vacation, Molly had researched the best places to take a boat to go dolphin watching. This would require us to drive through Savannah, so Molly requested that we stop there on the way back because there was a lot she wanted to see. This should not have been an unreasonable request. After all, we drove all this way and the least I could do was make a couple stops so my wife could enjoy some of the sights she wanted to.

We went dolphin watching and stopped for lunch. But once again, I got in the way. For some reason or another I allowed this event to become spoiled by the frustrations within me. As we passed through Savannah on our way back to St. Simons, I allowed my wife to find excuses to not stop because she could tell all I wanted to do was get back.

We finished the trip by taking three days to return home instead of two. I attempted to make up for my selfishness by finding fun things to do on the way back. I recalled stopping in St. Louis when I was a child and going to the top of the arch. I was secretly relieved to find out they were doing construction, and this adventure would not be possible this time. We made a stop in Kansas City and took the kids to the zoo. We all enjoyed seeing a koala for the first time and coming face to face with a kangaroo. I was glad this was something we all could share.

Trips to Oregon have yielded similar results. We watch as our children play in the ocean. Molly holds onto her excitement as she plans our itinerary. I mope along, waiting for some idea I conjured up in my mind to play out. But I'm not even sure what it would look like if it did come along. I find excuses to not do what Molly had hoped for, and I allow my family to suffer because of me. I wait for something better to come along, but I can't see that it is right there.

I now live for what I hope can happen, instead of enjoy what is happening in front of me. I ask myself if this is due to my depression. Is this the curse I have been given? I live my life trying to find what God's will is for me and for my family. How does he want me to raise my children? This remains in the forefront of my mind. Then comes my family. I live with a hope that I can provide for my family what they need and what they want. I wish for memories of fun times spent together. So why do I refuse to allow enjoyment? My desire is to spend time with my family and allow them to enjoy the time we have, but for some reason I don't let this happen.

Maybe I'm not so good at this faith, family, and fun thing after all.

9

"Not only so, but we also rejoice in our sufferings, because we know that suffering produces perseverance; perseverance, character; and character, hope." – *Romans 5:3-4.*

Many verses in the Bible are difficult to grasp, and this is one example. I'm not sure I can say with any confidence that I rejoice in my suffering. But perhaps this is why I write about hope. I suppose if there isn't any other good quality I possess, at least I can say I have perseverance. Or maybe I'm just stubborn.

I understand that the aforementioned verses, as well as every other Bible verse, must be taken in context. You must look at the audience, the context, and what precedes and follows the verse. And one of my pet peeves is when people take a verse out of context and apply it to their lives in order for it to fit the point they are trying to make. That said, I don't believe I am doing this passage any injustice by using it to emphasize what motivates me.

I'm not sure that most people would consider getting up in the morning to be an accomplishment, but much of the time it seems to take all my effort. When I have to get up for work in the morning, I despise the sound of my alarm, much like everyone else. On my days off, I lie in bed, knowing that I need to get up. I think of all the things I need and want to do. I hear my children playing or heading downstairs for breakfast, and think about how much I want to spend time with them. But I have absolutely no desire to get up.

I wish I had an inspirational reason to get out of bed in the morning. Or better yet, I wish I was just excited to get out of bed and get the day started. But I honestly don't know what gets me out of bed. Stubbornness, I guess. I get out of bed and go on with my day because that's what I do. I prefer to think that it's due to my perseverance; that makes me feel better.

Getting out of bed in the morning is a poor example of someone overcoming obstacles. Very few books on the subject exist. Motivational speakers don't give speeches to convince people to get out of bed in the morning. Hollywood will never create a movie that makes people tear up or get goosebumps when the main character finally gets the courage to throw the covers off and lazily roll out of bed, mumbling under his breath about how much he knows the day is going to suck. But each day that I wake up with breath in my body, I will continue to push forward with hope that God has a purpose for my life because I can't give up if I know God has a plan for me. I may not know what it is, but I continue to wait.

Each new day proves to be more difficult than the last. The hope from the previous night that I might wake up a different person is met with reality as the new day is met by the sun. Any optimism I may have had continues to dwindle as the day goes on. I beg and plead for some sort of relief, some sort of miracle. And I continue to wait.

Miracles are reserved for cheesy movies and inspirational songs. But I still hope for one nonetheless. I'm not sure what I'm waiting for, however. And I'm not sure why I feel I have anything to complain about or that anything is owed to me. I have a wife who's too good for me. I have three amazing children whom I love with everything in me. I have a nice house that backs up to a beautiful open space in the best state in the country. (Unless you're thinking of moving here, then it's an awful place to live). Looking at my life, I should be the happiest person in the world. So why aren't I?

To some people, I may seem to have it all together. I would like to think that I have accomplished quite a bit. But what I have didn't come easy. I spent ten years as a volunteer firefighter, trying to get hired full-time. Ten years focused on something other than my family. Ten years thinking that maybe this job will solve my issues and reduce my stress, at which time I will finally be able to enjoy my family. But when my time came, I had already been beaten down by the feeling of failure. I agree with the theory that each person has a baseline level of happiness, which would lead to the conclusion that no matter when I achieved this goal I set for myself, it was never going to result in ultimate happiness. This resulted in me revealing to my wife that I have accepted the fact that I will never really be happy.

I now see the same stress in my life that I once saw in my own father. As a kid, I wondered why he couldn't just relax. Now I fear my children look at me the same way, and I worry they will eventually succumb to the same stress. I still hope that some-day soon my anxiety and depression will vanish, and I will be able to enjoy my life, hopefully when I still have the chance to enjoy time with my family. My dad seems less stressed now. Maybe he figured out something I have yet to learn. Maybe it's because all of us children are now grown and out of the house. Maybe there's still hope for me.

The day my mom finally found out who I truly was, I was a senior in high school. I secluded myself in my bedroom as I had many times before. I found myself weeping uncontrollably for no reason. My mom heard and came into my room to check on me. When she asked what was wrong, I assured her that nothing was causing me to cry. I just felt like it. Mothers have a way of understanding their sons on a deeper level, and she knew I was being honest. But this honesty wasn't good news. She knew exactly what was wrong.

From the first time my mom was able to recognize there were battles going on inside of me, I have sought out help. However, the medications have proven to be more harm than good. I tried prescription after prescription without success. When I finally found something that altered my perception for the better, it either made me physically sick or so numb I no longer had compassion for anyone. And I would prefer to hold on to my love for others over the love I have for myself. So now I just continue through life the same way God made me the day I was born. Okay, maybe a little differently.

What we do doesn't make us who we are. And no matter what job I have, where I live, who my friends are, or who my family is, I will still be the same person inside. But I can work with the person I am inside to create the man God wants me to be. I believe that, in one way or another, God had His hand in making me the way I am, or at least knew how I would be, and I'm convinced it was for a reason. But if I sit by and let it overcome me, I have already lost. If I persevere until the end, however, who know what kind of man God desires for me to be?

"How do you like being a firefighter?"

"Best job in the world." This is the typical response to this question, and we remind ourselves constantly of how great our jobs are.

Walking into the grocery store after leaving the hospital on what felt like a typical day, my paramedic partner pointed out how atypical our jobs are. "In what other job do you take someone who's pulseless and not breathing, get pulses back, drop them off at the hospital alive, and then go grab lunch?" But we rely on these very infrequent instances to maintain us through all the difficult times. I can't recall all of the difficult calls I have been on, nor do I want to. Occasionally we talk about these calls with each other when something jogs our memory, but most of the time we keep to ourselves.

There is an ever-increasing number of firefighters committing suicide across the United States and the world. The assumption that an individual's happiness is related to possessions, family, financial status, employment, etc., is dangerous. We watch as firefighters, police officers, veterans, athletes, and celebrities commit suicide, and wonder how they could ever do such a thing. The general consensus is, "He had everything going for him. I'm not sure what could have lead to this."

My wife has voiced her concerns about my depression. I've explained to her that if she really knew my heart, she shouldn't have any concern at all. In order for someone to take their life, they first lose hope. Even though I don't rejoice in my suffering, I hold onto hope that good will endure. I hurt for each person lost by their own hand. I hurt knowing it wasn't prevented, as if I think in some way it's my responsibility. There is no way to describe this sorrow. It's a feeling of someone slipping through your fingers when you held on as best you could. Like when you performed CPR on a child and prayed that somehow the kid would make it, but she didn't. But if this is the way I feel, I can't imagine the sorrow that God must endure during these times.

But hope is not lost. It will prevail. I hold onto it as the weight of the world leaves me folded over both mentally and physically. I feel I will soon resemble a question mark more than I do a man. I'm weighed down by daily life and the unrelenting, uncontrollable thoughts that run through my mind. I continue to write as life tells me it's pointless and that anything I have to say isn't worth the time it takes to write it down.

There is an overwhelming sense of evil as I try to control my mind, when everything is telling me there is no point in finishing the book I started writing. But I continue to write because I hold onto the hope that perhaps this is what the Lord wants from me. Maybe this is why I am the way I am.

I press forward in writing this, and life continues to get more difficult. I have seen some of the hardest times in my life. Fake smiles are replaced by silent stares when friends and family attempt to converse with me. Questions from my wife are met with a quiet mumble as I can't seem to break the blank stare gazing toward nowhere, as though I'm looking for some answer beyond this world. Friends have passed away far too soon. Another celebrity suicide is in the news. Neighbors fight because of lies told by evil. The evil that feels the pressure of time, knowing that soon the battle will be over, and good will have won.

I'm not sure if I'm stubborn or persistent, but I feel the need to continue pressing forward. Maybe I still have hope that I will be able to make a difference. Maybe I still have hope that what I do is for a greater purpose, something bigger than myself. Maybe it's the Holy Spirit nudging me through each day. And if I have a purpose to continue working toward something greater than I can imagine, I will push forward to give others hope.

My story is not a cheerful one. I'm not about to pass along the secret of happiness. I don't conclude with a storybook ending. But I do hold onto hope. I hold onto hope because through my suffering I will continue to persevere. I hold onto hope because I know the story isn't over yet. I hold onto hope that I can give someone else hope. Hope that will see them through tomorrow and that together we will persevere. Hope that after this life is over, when there is no more sorrow, when there are no more tears, we will meet face to face.

"I have fought the good fight, I have finished the race, I have kept the faith." - *2 Timothy 4:7.*

10

Quite a while ago I started telling myself, "It's not about me." And as I began to accept that fact, life seemed to find new meaning. So why did I write a book about myself? I'm a nobody from nowhere, and my story isn't the same as yours. I have no idea the struggles you deal with, and I couldn't fix them if I did.

I didn't write about me because I live the way I believe you should. Remember: Learn from my mistakes rather than making your own! I have made plenty of them for both of us. You won't deal with all the same things I have dealt with, and vice versa. No two stories are the same. But this is your story. Own it. Take charge of it.

Life tends to not turn out the way we had imagined in childhood. But this is the life you have been gifted.

Make the best use of it. If you have, or ever had, or know someone who has ever had to deal with mental illness, you know how controlling it can be. But don't let it take hold of your life. If you deal with this every day, remember that you are meant to be more than your illness. How you live your life is up to you. There is no self-help book or motivational speaker more powerful than your determination. You can read every book on overcoming life's obstacles, listen to every motivational speech and inspirational song, and watch every uplifting movie, but if you choose to let life defeat you, you will be defeated.

If you live with determination and perseverance, and accept that life isn't about you but about serving others, your life is still going to be difficult. I hate to be the one to break it to you, but that's the way it is. However, you will find that life has a new purpose. A life lived to serve others is a life with meaning. It's a life worth living.

Goals will set you on the right path, but they are not the ultimate destination. If you live for wealth, a new job or promotion, more possessions, fame, or the next thing life has to offer, you will always want more. There is no amount of money, no magic number of friends, no maximum quantity of possessions that will satisfy. You will continue to feel empty. As C.S. Lewis wrote, "If I find in myself a desire which no experience in this world can satisfy, the most probable explanation is that I was made for another world."

So knowing that this life is lived for another still to come, plant your feet firmly on the path laid out for you by the Creator of all that is. Life will knock you off your feet. It will blow sand and dirt across your path so that it no longer seems to be visible. But if you get back up, broken and bruised, and plant your feet, your path will never cease to be lit.

Live your life with a sense of purpose. Live to be the friend people count on when their car breaks down or their house catches fire. Live to be the parent whose goal is to create memories for your children. Live to be the sibling who jumps into the deep end to pull out your brother who is calling for help. Live with the purpose of expanding the Kingdom of God. Live to show others that you love them more than you love yourself. Live for the life in the world beyond our own.

Live to give more than you get. Live to leave everything better than when you found it. Live for time with your family and your friends. Live to love more than you are loved. Live with a sense of hope in purpose because your life has more purpose than you can fathom. Live your life so that your future self can look back without regret. Live your life so that you will have no doubt about one day hearing your Father say to you, "Well done, my good and faithful servant."

I have made so many mistakes in my life. But I know those mistakes have taught me more than I will ever know. Those mistakes have been forgiven, and have lead me to where I am today. I press forward knowing that my life is not lived for myself. So the question I posed previously as to why I would write a book about myself was a little misleading. Although this has been the story of my life and struggles, I put it into words because I hurt when I see others who are lost and hurting. I hope they can learn from my mistakes before they lose control of their own lives. Perhaps my story can help someone who is lost. Perhaps my story can take someone who is on an uncertain path and redirect them to the path of hope. Perhaps that person is you.

ABOUT THE AUTHOR

Christopher Bussard is a firefighter in Colorado who has had the pleasure of serving the same community for more than 16 years. In 2017, he initiated his fire department's peer support program, which works with department members to help them with the stressors to which first responders are subjected. Christopher has battled with depression, anxiety, and obsessive-compulsive disorder his entire life, and he has a heart to help others who suffer with mental illness. In this book, he has combined this desire with his enjoyment of writing to encourage others who are struggling.

Christopher lives in northern Colorado with his wife and three children. Living in Colorado offers many opportunities to appreciate the world God created, and the author spends his time outside of work enjoying his family, woodworking, archery, hiking, and fishing.

Made in the USA
Lexington, KY
18 April 2019